Explorations in Teacher Training

Explorations
in
Teacher Training

– problems and issues

Edited by Tony Duff

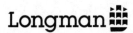

Longman Group UK Limited
Longman House, Burnt Mill, Harlow,
Essex CM20 2JE, England
and Associated Companies throughout the world

© Longman Group UK Limited 1988

First published 1988

Set in Linotron 10/12 Erhardt

Printed in Great Britain
by The Eastern Press Limited,
London and Reading

ISBN 0 582 03719 0

Introduction

This collection of essays celebrates twenty-five years of teacher training by the International House organisation. Its aim is to present a varied group of pieces about different aspects of teacher training and some of the issues and problems which arise. Although it is a celebration of one organisation's activities over a quarter of a century, it is hoped that the collection deals in a broad-based way with topics that are of general interest to people working in quite different institutions involved in the preparation and training of teachers. The papers come from various hands and reflect the views of trainers of teachers with great experience and different perspectives. It is not intended that the collection should provide answers to the very difficult questions which arise in the preparation of teachers or convenient formulae for running courses.

Neither is it the intention that this should be a comprehensive collection that takes account of all the different contexts to be found in the spectrum of teacher education throughout the world. Rather is the aim to present a collection of insights into some of the fundamental questions and, to some extent, to provide a record of how the work of one institution has developed in its first twenty-five years.

At this point, something must be said of the institution that is International House. It is an organisation that has always evoked strong feelings – pro and contra – among those who have trained as teachers with it, who have worked and work for it, and among other organisations in TEFL. It has sometimes been accused of being arrogant and self-absorbed. Such strong reactions are perhaps the price that must be paid by a body which has always tried to be challenging, questioning and innovative.

Strength of feeling has been generated not least by the International House "four-week course" and its influence, which has been formative in the development of the EFL profession. Other organisations – for example, the British Centre – have run short intensive courses for many years. However the enormous number of TEFL professionals throughout the world who took the International House short, intensive course as part of their training experience is quite remarkable; and the number of other courses for which in many important features it has served as a model is also striking.

A number of the articles at various points refer to the limitations and constraints of this initial intensive training course. Nevertheless, in terms of participant reaction to it, it is notable that the euphoric enthusiasm which the vast majority express about it as a totally stimulating experience contrasts sharply with the disappointment which many – often the same teachers, who have now worked in diverse institutions in the world at a different stage in their development – express about M.A. courses that they have followed.

One of the charges that has sometimes been laid at the door of International House is that it has "a method" from which no teacher must deviate, and indeed that there is an "IH teacher" (a myth at once rebutted and given some credence by Jeremy Harmer in his piece "Swinging in from a Chandelier", a title that both catches the spirit of a certain kind of enthusiasm at one moment in the development of International House and gently mocks it). The diversity of view expressed in the papers shows unequivocally that we are not celebrating twenty-five years of "the Method". The distorting transformation of Stanislavski's ideas about training actors into what was known in Hollywood in the 1950s as "Method Acting", as a result of half-understanding of what he was saying, is somewhat paralleled by the distortion involved in what some speak of as "the IH method".

The other most commonly levelled criticism of the approach to the training of teachers is that we are so busy being "practical" that we never stop to think about the assumptions, hypotheses, and principles – in effect, the "theory" – on which the practice is based. It is true that our emphasis is "applied" and there is even impatience with "theory" which does not have a clear relationship with practice. But the whole tradition of training at International House sprang from intelligent reflection on classroom practice in order to achieve what is now referred to as "principled decision-making" in practice. Trainers and teachers at International House have always been aware that the "unexamined (pedagogic) life is not worth living" and have been engaged in examining the life of language learning and teaching for a very long time. "Naïve realists" are important, as Denis Donoghue has written in a somewhat different, but related context: " . . . Theory is bound to come into it, but only as an imperfection and sometimes as an evil. I do not see much point in haggling with colleagues over theories of literature. Theory begins to matter only when it determines practice; prescribes it, predicts it, sets limits upon it. So: take the theories lightly until they darken into practice; then intervene."

The variety of view and approach evident in this collection reflects the organisation's capacity to accommodate diversity. Yet within that variety, it is notable how attitudes and values echo each other and share common ground.

If it is not the intention to provide answers, it is the hope that this collection will give the reader insight into how training has developed over twenty-five years and how resolving some of the difficulties has been approached, and continues to be explored. The intention is to share something of the experience with the reader – from the first pioneering courses to what has been involved in building the range that is run today.

Tony Duff

Acknowledgements

International House would like to express its appreciation to the authors who have contributed to this celebratory collection.

I am very grateful to my secretary, Elsa Gordon, for the care and skill with which she typed the manuscript. T.D.

Contents

1

John Haycraft gives us a picture of the impetus behind the first teacher-training courses which he and his wife, Brita, began in order to provide properly prepared staff for the school of English which they set up in London in 1959.

Today, when there is very considerable diversity of training available and training has developed the wider perspectives which include teacher education and development, it is often forgotten just how significant a pioneering step these courses of training for teachers of English as a foreign language were. There were in existence one-year PGCE courses within a number of universities, notably London, Bangor, and Leeds. But their emphasis tended to be on the philosophy of education with much less weight being given to the actual business of the teacher working in the classroom. It was not uncommon for teachers in training to be observed no more than once or twice by supervisors during the academic year. The extent to which student-teachers still feel this lack of practical work on many state courses is borne out by the common remark, "I've learnt more in the last few weeks than I did in my whole three years at teacher training college . . . ".

To some extent the model for the short, sharp training course which the Haycrafts set up came from the world of business and industry, where training has always had a strong, applied bias. In industry the benefits of intensive, sharply focused training were recognised early on, along with the highly motivating impact which such experience frequently has on the participants. The proliferation of short, intensive courses in all areas of life and work – personal development, time management, counselling, computer science, to mention only the most conspicuous – suggests that the benefits are indeed considerable.

John Haycraft has always emphasised the primacy of the direct, the practical, the effective, and the supreme importance of human contact in teaching and learning, and these are qualities which he sees as remaining fundamental to the process of training teachers.

The First International House Preparatory Course – an historical overview

JOHN HAYCRAFT

Let me make an obvious statement, which like many of its kind is often forgotten: training is most effective when urgently needed and when the reasons for this urgency are clear.

Have you ever met someone who learnt a language for Army

Intelligence, years ago, during the war? In a short time, many were trained to interrogate fluently in another language, while others learnt to translate effectively. The urgency was there and the objectives were evident.

Why do we want to train teachers for EFL? For what? For whom? How often do we ask ourselves these questions when planning a course?

Are we aware how often answers are affected by the "prestige factor"? The problem may be the instinct and taste for prestige which welcome an eminent professor simply because "everyone has heard of him". "It is the honour of having you here that is important," said the organiser of a medical conference in Ancona to an English friend of mine, a well-known professor of medicine, who had just given a lecture in English to an audience which only understood Italian, but nevertheless applauded him vociferously.

There is also the "prestige theme". After all, it is so unexciting to give a course full of simple platitudes, which are precisely what trainees most need. I remember in a South American country an impoverished Ministry of Education paying for a professor of linguistics to come from England to lecture to three thousand teachers, assembled in the capital at vast expense. What these teachers really needed was to improve their English and to learn how to teach forty students in a class – not to listen to a theoretical lecture isolated from the realities of practice. The Emperor's clothes is one of the truest of folk legends.

In the birth pangs of the EFL profession in 1962, we were very lucky. We started teacher training because we desperately needed teachers who could give effective lessons to adult multilingual classes in which verbal communication was difficult. Little or no practical training for the classroom teaching of EFL then existed, so we had to set about designing a short intensive course, somewhat on the lines of the kind of training that was then beginning to be used in business and industry, and to teach it ourselves.

Our teachers needed to know how to build their lessons on whatever English had already been taught, relate new vocabulary to objects brought into the classroom and other visual aids. Trainees had to learn how to mime and communicate dramatically and use the kind of situational context which would be relevant to our students' language needs. And of course, they had to learn as much as possible about English grammar and pronunciation, seen from the foreigner's point of view.

This last was particularly difficult as the British are still the only nation which is not taught its own grammar or pronunciation at school.

We were aware after six years English language teaching in Spain and training teachers in Sweden, plus three years with multilingual classes in London, that the presentation of English grammar had to be focused on comparative differences between the languages spoken by foreign students.[1]

In those days, twenty-five years ago, the major textbooks available were Eckersley's *Essential English*, and an Australian book, called *Situational English*. There was also Bill Allen's (W. Stannard Allen) *Living English Structure*, which gave a straightforward and coherent analysis of English grammar from the foreign learner's point of view as did his *Living English Speech* for basic English pronunciation. These last two books were godsends, not only for teaching foreign students, but also for introducing trainee teachers to these areas.

At that time, the EFL profession hardly existed, and private schools were regarded generally as rackets, in which untrained undergraduates figured prominently in part-time jobs on summer courses. Those who taught EFL frequently had the attitude: "I'm English, aren't I? So I can teach my own language, can't I?" Those people with English degrees were particularly confident because of their qualification, but were apparently unaware that *Beowulf*, the Venerable Bede and *King Lear* are not much help in teaching multiple nationalities in a beginners' class.

There was also a feeling that it was not language but literature that was important. I remember meeting the same attitude in another context when learning Russian at school and being confronted with Pushkin's *The Captain's Daughter*, on the first day – and nothing else. In EFL, it was difficult to convince proponents of the "literature school" that it is not easy to read great books in English without knowing the language, and that if one is going to teach how to read it, it is also possible to combine it with the speaking and listening skills, which most students come to Britain for.

Up to 1962, my wife Brita and I had tackled the question of training our teachers by observing classes, giving advice, encouraging, and suggesting different approaches. This was early in-service training – or learning on the job – and the process could well take months. As International House grew, it was necessary to find a more effective form of induction.

Our first teacher-training course began one sunny September morning in 1962 with ten people who had answered advertisements in the *New Statesman* and *The Times* personal column. Because we had

---

[1]   It took a long time for grammarians to realise this distinction. Even in the late 1970s, grammar books for foreign students were produced with an approach based on the needs of the English learner.

no idea if there would be a demand, the course was to last only two weeks.

The actual design of the course was not difficult because, as I have said, our needs were clear. The object was to give the trainees as much practical grounding and exposure to the classroom as possible. Much of this meant, as it were, teaching communication in an unfamiliar situation.[1] The questions confronting us were: how could we ensure that trainees would absorb many new ideas and techniques in a very short space of time? How to ensure that students were taught spoken English, which was their first priority? How to make the language learnt memorable? How to involve all the students in classroom activities? How to ensure variety of approach even when teaching and revising the same areas of language? How to present and consolidate new language? How to make students feel at ease and interested? We were fortunate in our environment because it was easy to involve our trainees with other activities in our school of English and give them a real sense of being part of a functioning organisation. Here, trainees could meet those whom they might ultimately teach, become involved in the educational problems, and learn in a realistic atmosphere. Later, it also had the advantage that the trainers themselves continued to teach EFL, thus keeping up-to-date with new methods and text books. (A specimen timetable for the second week of the course appears on the next page.)

Indeed the extent to which our practical emphasis was revolutionary to some – with teaching practice taking place every day – is reflected in the following story: I remember once, going to the Ministry of Education, as it then was, and meeting a supercilious lady who was known by her colleagues as "the tennis ball in the rain-pipe" – because she blocked everything. When I remarked that teacher training in the state system might be more effective if properly integrated into the new comprehensive schools, which were then being created, rather than being carried out in separate colleges, she raised both eyebrows and said loftily: "Mr Haycraft, do you realise you are criticising the entire educational system in the U.K.?" "Yes, Miss G., I do," I replied. Our discussion ended rapidly.

The outline we designed for the course has in its essentials proved effective to this day. In the morning, we gave seminars in which we discussed principles of teaching and their practical application to the

---

[1]   It is interesting how the part of the course which deals with communication skills can be used for other forms of training. A trainer of ours, back from the States, told me he was making a fortune using the same technique in training employees of a large video company.

	Monday	Tuesday	Wednesday	Thursday	Friday
AM Lectures/ seminars on language methodology 2 hours	How to practice language: – drills – how to prompt using visual aids	Going over lesson plans with trainees for today's TP (3rd session of lesson planning) The "free" stage	Language laboratory visit/ session checking of lesson-plans/ peer teaching	Using drama with EFL students	Use of readers; activities to get students to read. Setting up a class library
1 hour	Analysis of the Present Perfect (1)	Stress: in long words	Analysis of Present Perfect (2)	Intonation: practice in identifying "tones"; use of the fall-rise	Review of the week's work
PM Teaching practice (TP) + discussion of lessons (including with the EFL students	everyday ⟶				
	followed by observation of teachers in the school				
	Example of a timetable for the second week of an International House three-week course in the 1960s				

classroom. This included oral drills and the use of the tape recorder, which was then a new teaching aid.[1]

The seminars also dealt with grammar and pronunciation. As it was obviously impossible to go through the entire system of grammar in a two-week course, I concentrated on various major problems, such as the Definite Article and Present Perfect. In the process, we broke up the language into short "presentation formulae" to be taught at various stages. We then moved to ways of presenting and practising them. It was this actual process which was most important, and we hoped that

[1]   Language laboratories had only become available in Britain in the early 1960s. There was little material for them until Alan Wakeman, who ran the language laboratories at International House, published his *English Fast* in 1967.

trainees would learn to apply it to other language structures they had to teach. On the pronunciation side, Brita made trainees aware above all of word and sentence stress and ways of correcting the commonest sound mistakes, such as *o, w* and *th*.

Our approach was based on giving trainees the enthusiasm and *savoir faire* to explore further, once they had started teaching. Even today, I warn new trainees that, at the end of one of our four-week courses, they will, as it were, only be outside Paddington Station when their destination is Plymouth. Even if they have not got very far, one hopes they are on the railway lines and going in the right direction.

Following these seminars, which aimed at a maximum level of participation from trainees and at making them think, we had teaching practice for two hours every afternoon with "guinea pig" classes. Our students were only too happy to have extra, free tuition, although after a time, we realised that it was essential to charge a nominal fee as otherwise students attended irregularly. But these practice lessons provided (and still do so) the opportunity for students, especially those from developing countries and refugees, to enjoy inexpensive tuition, which was effective and often of a very high standard. "Guinea pig" classes are particularly helpful to students for revision and recycling. What we had discussed the previous day was prepared by trainees as homework.

Teaching practice is the essential stage of application of principles and allows the key process of trainee teachers "trying things out" to take place. On this first course, trainees taught for ten minutes, which was followed by a further ten minutes comment on the teaching from trainer and trainees. The foreign students also participated in this criticism which was valuable, if often simple, like: "Write on blackboard bad".

If applied out of the blue today in a large teaching establishment, the prospect of this kind of teaching practice would probably seem so alarming that it would never be introduced. Since, however, we were beginning on a small scale and were breaking new ground, it was accepted without question by the trainees, even if sometimes it made them tremble.

Twelve years later, I went to an IATEFL conference and saw a talk advertised on something I had never heard of before: "micro-teaching". When I enquired what it was, I was given an exact description of our teaching practice. Thus, can new things be discovered independently all over the world and be given special names to lend them status and significance.

Practice was based on mutual, supportive criticism which is usually an ugly word because associated with malice. However, we ensured that everyone realised that criticism could be helpful. It started with the good points, making any negative ones which followed more acceptable. Thus, these sessions came to resemble showing a short story or novel to a friend for frank comment, which is usually of value. Throughout International House, there was a further effect of stimulating discussions about teaching. Our staff, who ultimately all went through this process, also came to welcome in-service observation of their classes. In fact, we would actually get our teachers complaining if they were not observed regularly. They would request observation when they had difficulties or wanted to try something new. Very different it was from the suspicious guarding of new teaching ideas, common to many staff rooms at that time.

After teaching practice, observation of classes in the school followed for two hours every day. Even if standards were not as high in some classes as they were once all the teachers had taken the course, they were valuable in giving trainees experience of the EFL classroom, and confronting them with some of the problems that arise. It also stimulated trainees to ask themselves how they would deal with a situation if they disagreed with how it had been handled by the teacher they observed.

Intensive the course certainly was – and still is. Its fifty hours were the equivalent of half a term at a university, crammed into two weeks. Because of this intensity, trainees were absorbed into an unfamiliar world, so different from other forms of teaching they were likely to have experienced. Also, it forced us to make the course as stimulating and varied as we could. Even if trainees worked hard, they seemed to enjoy it.

It came to be accepted that hierarchy and status were barriers to communication. I had spent a post-graduate year at the Yale Drama School, and our atmosphere was very much that of a team in a theatre, rehearsing, discussing, acting out, but with the additional vital ingredient of mixing with other nationalities. There was a feeling that this was not work because everyone was so involved in preparing for that ultimate dénouement: effective teaching practice, into which were drawn the awakening skills produced by seminars, observation of classes, and the formative comments made on previous teaching practice.

As further courses followed on the success of the first, the outrage of those outside in the big world of education, who felt that only universities and colleges should run teacher training, could be heard. Once, Sidney Stevens, the founder of BBC English by Radio, came up to me to express his horror. "How can you run a teacher training course of only two weeks?" he asked indignantly. "Well, what alternative is there?" I exploded. "No one else runs any courses for the classroom. Isn't it better to do something? How else can one recruit teachers who have some idea of how to teach EFL?"

One of the disadvantages of being in a totally new profession was that all sorts of associated, but essentially different, ideas were applied to it. A university degree was regarded as essential, although no degree prepared for the difficulties we were faced with, even if it did give a valuable educational background. In fact, later, when training people for Voluntary Service Overseas, we found that school-leavers were usually more suited to EFL, initially, at any rate, than university graduates. School-leavers had fewer fixed ideas about learning and teaching, and were less likely to verbalise excessively. They found it easier to adapt to sharply focused objectives, the essentially practical tenets of our classroom methodology, the need to present language simply and clearly, and to consolidate by encouraging the students to express themselves.

As we ran more courses to satisfy the demand from people wanting to be trained, it was also necessary to find work opportunities for them and career outlets. A school in Sardinia asked me for a teacher, so I recommended a woman who had shown promise. The result was disastrous. The woman complained that she had been exploited, and the school that the woman was hopeless and aggressive. I vowed that this would not happen again. So began the system of schools affiliated to International House, which now number eighty in twenty countries. Through this scheme, we sent teachers only to schools we had vetted and visited regularly. We gave the schools the educational help they needed and kept them up-to-date with new ideas and materials through regular conferences. Many of the directors came on training courses, while teachers of ours opened new schools which then became affiliated.

In selecting teachers we also found that the training course was an invaluable way of getting to know prospective teachers for places as varied as Rome, Lisbon, Libya, Algiers and Beirut. From the personality revealed on teaching practice, we could gauge much more about reactions to different countries than simply from references and interviews. In fact, without the training courses we could probably never have staffed our schools abroad satisfactorily.

As it grew, teacher training became a cornerstone of the whole developing structure of International House, reminiscent again of the interlinking I had seen at the Yale Drama School. There, student playwrights had produced plays which were acted by student actors, directed by student directors, with lighting and scenery also created by students, with feedback from questionnaires at the end of each play.

At International House, trainees wanted to know more about our foreign students because they hoped to teach them. They wanted to plumb their skills and errors in speaking English, their learning attitudes, their educational background. These students, in turn, were anxious to meet native speakers, particularly as in London they always complained that it was difficult to meet them. A social programme grew up with activities such as Conversation Exchange, English through Acting, and Pronunciation Workshops where both trainees and foreign students took part – all with the aim of encouraging participation.

Gradually, we provided enough teachers for our needs, and the courses became a general way of entering EFL as a profession. Those who did well on courses would teach mainly abroad for a year or two as virtual apprentices before becoming fully professional teachers, and then often went on to become Directors of Studies, teacher trainers, and perhaps do a post-graduate degree.

As the courses grew and developed, teacher training was established in International House affiliates abroad, and dealt more specifically with the particular national problems. There was also a greater degree of administrative consolidation. As EFL itself has developed, new topics and approaches have been introduced while others have been thrown out. But the vase is still the same, even if the flowers are different.

Above all, the values of friendliness, a sense of equality, sharing, and sympathy for other people's problems, have remained. Now, there are special courses for foreign teachers, including one lasting three months, a recently developed course for trainers, and another for teachers of Business English, together with a distance training programme for the RSA Diploma in TEFLA (Correspondence Course).

In our twenty-five years, we have trained over twenty thousand potential teachers. As Jeremy Harmer wrote recently in the *EFL Gazette*: "Hands up those EFL teachers who did not start their careers training at International House." In 1978, I ended an article for A. J. Hornby's Festschrift by saying it was time someone lent us a hand. Shortly afterwards, Steve Walters of the Bell Educational Trust asked me if I would welcome an RSA certificate at initial training level. It would mean that the RSA would adopt our syllabus, and that other people could more easily run training courses of the type we had developed over the years. I agreed because I have never felt that teacher training should be the monopoly of one organisation.

Today, the pattern of the four-week course is followed all over the world, with a generally recognised certificate. Now, there is no need to go to desperate lengths to find teachers who can use the special methodology which learners who know little English need.

2   Jeremy Harmer introduces some vivid recollections from nine people who, between 1973 and 1987, took the course at International House London, with the provocative title "Swinging in from a Chandelier". This constellation of reminiscences highlights some of the key questions that have been asked about the nature of the course and indeed some of the major criticisms that have been made of it. Most significant among these are: the brevity of the course and the degree of pressure which participants undergo and the extent to which this may favour certain personalities and put others at an extreme disadvantage. Roger Gower in his plea for a more radical basis of course organisation addresses this problem directly and argues the importance of providing trainees with time and space to reflect in (see "Are Trainees Human?", page 24). One of the strongest criticisms that has been levelled at the course is that it is a "cloning system" dedicated to producing the "International House type teacher" who has been pulverised into existence by rigid trainers who will admit of no questioning of their dogmas.

Clearly an institution like International House has a recognisable "house style"; those being trained on initial courses need a fairly distinct framework within which to operate and also need reasonably secure guidelines, which indeed help to reduce the level of pressure. If allowed to go too far, such tendencies do run the risk of solidifying into dogma and not giving sufficiently free rein to individual instincts. But the initial training course from its first inception was planned as a base for teachers to work from and to develop the insight which they may have gained from it in their own ways, not as a definitively forming process. As Jeremy Harmer points out, many of today's most "prominent figures in the world of EFL" experienced their first training at International House and the diversity of their development – and that of International House-trained teachers working at so many institutions throughout the world – is perhaps the best answer to this criticism.

Swinging in from a Chandelier

Reminiscences of preparatory training courses

JEREMY HARMER

Introduction

Most people who have done an initial four-week teacher-training course at some stage of their career in EFL have strong memories of the experience. They will often remember events on the course vividly, even after the passage of a considerable amount of time. Part of this is obviously due to the exposure to new ideas and practices, part is clearly due to the pressure of any short course, and part is attributable to the fact that the four-week course comes (for many teachers) at the beginning of their careers.

The four-week course is now of course geared towards the attainment of the preparatory certificate from the Royal Society of Arts. Courses for this certificate are offered in many EFL centres throughout the UK and abroad. But the concept of the four-week intensive teacher-training programme to prepare EFL teachers grew from the training work of International House which, since the first course in 1962, has trained more than 20,000 teachers. Many of them are now prominent figures in the world of EFL, and most reputable institutions that are staffed by British teachers will have a proportion of International House trained men and women "at the chalkface".

Many suggestions are now being made about the content of such courses, about their shortcomings and their strengths, and about changes that might be instigated. The syllabus is being re-examined and the underlying philosophy behind intensive teacher training is being questioned. Most of this questioning takes place, of course, in conversations between trainers and course designers and it is they who will determine the future of short courses.

In this article, however, I want to approach an evaluation of the initial four-week teacher-training course from an entirely different angle. I want to investigate what it feels like from the "consumer's" point of view. How do trainees feel about the experience? What do they remember about it and how much has it influenced their teaching?

Method

Nine trainees were interviewed about their feelings and experiences. They are titled A-J and can be described as follows (f=female, m=male):

A(f) did the course in 1973 after two years as a teacher of handicapped children.

B(m) did the course in 1974. He had already been teaching EFL for a year when he did this.

C(m) did the course in 1978. With a PGCE he had been teaching modern languages at secondary level for three years.

D(f) did the course in 1979 after working for some time as an untrained EFL teacher.

E(m) did the course in 1980. He had no previous teaching experience.

F(m) did the course in 1985 and had no previous teaching experience.

G(f) did the course in 1985. With a PGCE in languages she had previously been teaching in Morocco.

H(m) was halfway through his 1987 course when he took part in this study. He had previously been teaching EFL in Switzerland.

J(f) was halfway through her 1987 course when she took part in this study. She had a PGCE and had been teaching home economics in a secondary school for two years.

Apart from F, all the participants recorded an interview in which they talked about their experiences. A and B were interviewed together, but otherwise the interviewees spoke with the interviewer alone.

The conversations were informal but the following two questions were always asked:

1. What did you like about the course?
2. What didn't you like about the course?

The conversations developed from the participants' answers to these questions.

Listening to the tapes afterwards, the most immediately obvious characteristic of the interviews was the similarity of many of the comments and reactions – whether the interviewees had done the course in the early 70s or nearer the present. The same preoccupations and feelings emerge constantly, some of them positive, others negative and unhappy. But because this was not in any sense a scientific study such reactions can not be subjected to rigorous statistical analysis. Instead, these reminiscences and comments are presented here through the words of the interviewees themselves.

"Very inspiring and motivating"

There is no doubt about the overall enthusiasm that participants felt about the course. As E said:

> I hadn't taught before so it was a new experience for me. It was very stimulating, very motivating. I felt that I'd learnt a lot . . . very good examples of how to teach at the time. That was the main thing. Very inspiring and motivating.

This sentiment was frequently echoed by the other trainees, and something of the excitement that many have felt on the course was communicated by B:

For me it was a complete change of orientation . . . the course was my first . . . putting into practice on a daily basis what you're learning . . . I can't compare it with anything else I've done where you're given something and you immediately go off and use it. So it's like here is a way to do something, try it, bit nervous, and you go into the classroom and you're actually trying it within half-an-hour sometimes.

The sense of immediacy and the organisation of the course obviously contribute to what another teacher, F, described as " . . . lots of adrenalin" and although, as we shall see, this contributes to very real feelings of stress and pressure, it has also given the course some of its excitement.

One feature that was frequently commented on was the teacher-training methodology. G summed it up as:

They used the same kind of methods to teach you as they expected you to use to teach other people.

and A eloquently summed up her reaction to the teaching style:

I'd never been in a classroom situation before where I wasn't just sitting there passively taking pearls of wisdom from, you know, the front of the class. For the first time somebody was involving me all the way through, asking me questions, keeping me with them. Having to put it into practice immediately was I found nerve-wracking but at the same time exciting . . .

"How little I knew"

It became clear that trainees who had taught before had a greater credibility problem to deal with. However, F, who had taught before, remarked that the teacher with the most experience in his group "did worst". Whether or not this is a common occurrence, it is certainly the case that trainees with experience have some difficulties to face. As C said:

It really made me realise how little I knew about teaching . . . thinking about myself . . . positioning, use of language in the class-room . . . The first week I felt my ego had gone. I started looking at myself . . . thinking about things I hadn't considered before.

C recovered from this feeling however, whereas H, in the middle of a course, was feeling unhappy at the time of the interview:

What I'm not enjoying is the stress and the feeling that I'm not really competent at things that I hoped I was competent at already.

Clearly, however, if the ego can survive there is much to be gained:

> I really liked the complete revelation that it was to me, all these
> wonderful new methods and wonderful new techniques for doing
> this job that I had had before. (D)

"Doing the right thing"

One of the achievements that is claimed for the four-week course
is its ability to send someone directly into an EFL classroom after
four weeks having given them the tools of survival, a situation that B
obviously recognises:

> There is a tendency to approach a novel situation where you don't
> know what to do and you don't know what to expect as going back
> to the basics and I think the International House course is really
> the basics – and that's what was so good about it. It gave you the
> confidence to go in and say "I've got something to do".

For G this feeling is expressed as:

> . . . confidence in the classroom and being confident of "Yes I am
> doing the right thing".

Many International House graduates, too, would recognise the lasting
effect of such a high pressure survival course:

> The whole of my teaching is heavily influenced by what happened in
> those four weeks; from simple things like the mechanics of drilling
> to making a substitution table which has 7 items . . . and then check
> questions and concept questions . . . (B)

"A nice learning atmosphere"

Many of the interviewees commented on their tutors and on their fellow
trainees. Overwhelmingly, they felt positive about their mentors:

> The teacher trainers basically created a nice learning atmosphere. (C)
>
> The teachers we've had have just been great, really. I mean they've
> instilled enthusiasm. (J)
>
> A lot of (the course's success) was to do with the personality of the
> teacher trainers. They were enthusiastic about teaching and therefore
> that rubbed off on the trainees. Because it was a new subject I felt
> I was learning a lot of new and interesting things and they were put
> across very clearly . . . (E)

This almost universal admiration is sometimes qualified, however. B
thought the tutors were:

The most dictatorial people I've ever met in my life in some ways, but they had to be because if someone goes off at tangents and you've got lots of personal anecdotes of classroom experience coming in you can't get down to the nitty-gritty.

Trainers have two functions, of course. They give input sessions, but they also give feedback on the trainees' teaching practice sessions. F thought that he was "very nicely helped and criticised" but two of the interviewees felt that the trainers were, if anything, too nice:

> Even if you did an absolutely dire lesson they'd say "Oh, this was quite good". They'd very rarely say "well that was terrible". (G)

> I think there were moments when they overemphasised the positive because there was something negative coming up . . . what you'd like is well that was nice but then let's get on to the nitty-gritty, because in a couple of weeks' time I'm going to be out there in front of real students. (B)

Often, however, it was the trainees themselves who gave themselves the most powerful feedback:

> There was only one lesson which was an absolute disaster and it sticks in my mind to this very day . . . the next day I did a very safe lesson. It was dead centre just as they said. (A)

"Everyone had the same problem"

Part of the success or failure of the four-week course depends upon the class of trainees – how well they work together and what kind of attitude they have to the task in hand and to each other. Here again the feeling was generally positive:

> There was this bonhomie – this sharing . . . everyone had the same problem: what do I do, how do I do it? (B)

> Our group has worked extremely nicely together . . . (there is a) lack of competitiveness. (J)

> It's not competitive with each other but the preoccupation with grades is very strong . . . It's not a question of "Oh God, I've got to do better than so-and-so" – at least not overtly anyway. (H)

> . . . and the interacting between trainees – there was a very good atmosphere in the group. (E)

Working together does have its pitfalls, however. Many trainees have experienced the member of their group who destroys a carefully worked-out plan:

You can have some really good ideas and know exactly what you want to do and organise it all with your group. But if someone else in your group decides after you've organised it all to go home and change it all it's going to muck up everybody else's . . . (J)

There's always the one guy – it's usually a guy – that's decided he'll do this and then goes and does something completely different. (G)

"Lots of adrenalin"

On one issue all the interviewees were agreed:

I hadn't realised quite how exacting it was going to be (C)

Everyone was . . . very intimidated by T(eaching) P(ractice) and worrying about that all the time – quite a lot of anxiety. (D)

F remarked that the pressure of the course produced "lots of adrenalin", especially during TP where they "put you on the spot". For H the pressure – halfway through the course – was proving very uncomfortable:

I don't like the permanent worry associated with fear involved with doing this course.

In one of the only really critical comments about a tutor D said:

That's a very strong memory, a personal feeling about it was . . . I had a lot of anxiety, a lot of stress about TP and the tutor didn't deal with that ever. He didn't actually recognise that I had it, let alone deal with it.

For most trainees the pressure of the course was directly related to its short duration:

The time period is . . . very short to cram all this in, plus to actually kind of integrate all the information and to put it into practice is practically impossible. (H)

It's the time element . . . I find there's just not enough time to stop and think . . . you've got so many ideas coming to you all the time. You're trying to put all these ideas into practice on your TPs. Initially you're doing it without the ideas so you're doing your own things and by the time you've got the new ideas you want to have a go, you want to stop and think about it; you want to have another go and change it . . . you just cannot be perfect straight away, it's going to take time and you just wish you could have more time to practise lots of different strategies for one skill, say, . . . and you keep thinking "OK well I might muck it up all the time until the end of the course, but if you'd given me a bit more time I might have found my way." There's no incubation period for thinking through your ideas. (J)

E spoke for everybody when he looked back on his course and remarked:

> The pressure, particularly of teaching practice, was very heavy . . . I
> wondered if there was any way of reducing that.

but then went on to say:

> Because you're under some kind of pressure it does spur you on –
> a lot of it is to do with that, I think, so it has a positive side to it
> as well.

How are we to assess the pressure that all International House trainees have felt? Is it a cause of disintegration or a force for good? A has no doubts:

> I learnt about pressure, enjoyment, and learning . . . people can take
> a lot of pressure if it's delivered in an enjoyable way, a rewarding way
> and you feel you are learning. Then I think people can take enormous
> pressure and I think those are the elements that I think I've still got
> left in my teaching . . . to try and inject energy into the students to
> take pressure; to try and make it enjoyable and to prove to them that
> learning is taking place.

And A, despite the fact that a personal relationship crumbled under the onslaught, said:

> It (the course) did call for commitment – but you always knew it
> was four weeks, you always knew there was a deadline somewhere
> and there was always this carrot of a payoff of a job. You know you
> really felt that you could get a job at the end of it.

A conjured up visions of trainees working long into the night over their lesson plans, but some resist this commitment:

> I want to just limit my hours of doing it even if it means a slightly
> worse result for me on the course, because you know last week and
> some of this week I was just working day and night and it never went
> out of my head and I found that the result I was getting in TP didn't
> really warrant it. So I thought I'll clock in at 8 and I'll clock off at 6
> and if I do well, great, and if I don't do well I won't be in permanent
> stress. (H)

But then some trainees feel more relaxed and rely on non-teaching friends to take part of the strain:

> I was living in a squat in Finsbury Park with some friends . . . they
> kind of took the pressure off. I'd come home and they'd help me
> create dialogues and they'd all sit around with a bottle of whisky and
> draw the appropriate visual aids. (G)

"Someone gave me a textbook"

One area that excited critical comment from trainees was their feeling that they had been let down in the area of textbooks (a feeling shared by trainees from the early 70s as well as by those from the 1980s):

> It was a sin to use a book, whereas in most teaching situations, particularly if you're teaching abroad, you're following a coursebook and you've got to kind of dip into it now and again or have something to do with it. (G)
>
> (1985)

> The day I started work someone gave me a textbook and I'd had no idea on the course that institutions existed with textbooks . . . I was not allowed in some senses to use a textbook. No one even suggested "go to a textbook, steal the idea, modify it slightly." It must come out of your own head . . . And whilst this is good when the textbook doesn't suit you, if you're forced into using a textbook, the students have bought it, etc etc, how to cope with it, make it interesting, make it varied . . . (is important). (B)
>
> (1974)

A felt the same lack on her course, but obviously manages perfectly well with her own material:

> We weren't encouraged to use textbooks and I'm still suffering from that . . . because I still find it easier to produce my own material than go from somebody else's because I don't know where they're going to, whatever, but . . . there are times when I think, "God, I wish I had the confidence to go in and just say right I'm going to use this textbook" and feel that I really knew how to exploit it, which I still don't.
>
> (1973)

"Sitting back to back with your legs round your neck"

Most trainees resist the disciplines of the four-week course to some extent, and many feel that they are oppressed by the "IH method". Thus A remembers her course and the idea that:

> . . . if you didn't swing in from a chandelier you couldn't make your mark, and quiet teachers weren't really up to it . . .
>
> (1973)

G, a 1985 trainee, seemed to be suggesting that things had not changed much:

> There's an IH way of doing it which is better if you're sitting back-to-back with your legs round your neck than if you're facing each other.

This is an hour and it's got to be a perfect little hour with a little peak where everybody learns, and then wind down to a game. And of course when you're seeing people three times a week, you don't have to really. You know you can . . . stop something and say "we'll finish it next time" which is really good 'cos they all come in . . . dead enthusiastic to get that finished . . . it's not the end of the world. But it would have been really quite the end of the world on the course . . .

(1985)

Conclusions

What is impressive, listening to these tapes, is the degree of involvement in the course that trainees feel – sometimes 14 years later. There is no doubt that at many levels most of them suggest that they gained enormously from the experience (although both J and H reserved judgement on that, quite naturally!).

That the same preoccupations exist now as there existed for many years is also noticeable. Pressure – and how to cope with it – emerges time and again as a major issue. Some people, like A, see it as a thoroughly positive force. Others find it excruciating. Worries about textbooks and the phantom "IH method" ring true across the years. And now, as then, the question has to be whether the limitations of the course and the "cloning" of the typical IH teacher that some commentators unkindly refer to (and in which there is certainly an element of truth) are outweighed by the course's ability to turn out enthusiastic survivors, equipped to start a promising career. Those of us who have done the International House four-week course will have experienced flashes of sympathetic recognition at the feelings and reactions of these nine trainees. It is a measure of the achievement of the International House trainers that there are so many of us.

Note

I am extremely grateful to Tony Duff and Gillie Cunningham who helped to make this study possible. And of course I would like to record my gratitude to the interviewees who gave of their time and experience to talk about their courses.

3   Roger Gower asks if trainees are human. Through this question
he wants to express his concern at the "techniquery" – the
emphasis on so-called methodology – which is to be found
on so many teacher-training courses – and to express his
dissent from it. The word "training" is the give-away. Just as
language teaching was dominated for many of its most formative
years by a behaviourist view of learning, so many approaches
to the preparation of teachers have been unduly dominated
by procedures, techniques, and "activities" that tend to have a
manipulative effect on learning.

Gower argues that it is not enough to deal with "basic,
classroom skills" and language awareness as many courses do,
but that trainees and students must be treated as individual
human learners and allowed to develop their pedagogic and
linguistic potential in fairly free course structures. He is proposing
some significantly different assumptions from which to plan and
organise courses, but at another and simpler level he is appealing
to a very old and primary axiom of teacher preparation: that
teachers must, as a first duty and prerequisite, be interested in
their students as people and genuinely take their personalities
into account when teaching. A view resonating in John Haycraft's
article where he says: "Above all, the values of friendliness, a sense
of equality, sharing, and sympathy for other people's problems,
have remained."

Are Trainees Human?

ROGER GOWER

Most pre-service ELT training courses set out with two principal
aims: they try to create an awareness of language – against the kind
of perspective thought necessary for teaching it in the classroom –
and they try to acquaint trainees with some basic classroom skills, a
few techniques, and methods currently in use. Short courses of four
to five weeks (full-time) or six to nine months (part-time), leading to,
for example, the Royal Society of Arts Preparatory Certificate, usually
blend "language work" with methodology in a very tightly organised
programme, which combines instruction from course tutors with
practice teaching by trainees.

To allow for micro-teaching, the number of trainees on each course
is usually small (12–18) while the number of trainers is relatively
large. Fees have to remain reasonable and so, training centres (both

in the public and independent sectors) rarely regard courses as hugely profit-making. On the other hand, teacher-training activity gives a school a certain prestige, particularly among teachers. For those who work on the courses, the experience can provide valuable "teacher development" and indeed "career development" opportunities – an attractive alternative to the conventional classroom routine. Servicing the profession in this way is not only a good thing in itself, it can revitalise a school (that is, until the training process too becomes routine and new ruts are established!) It can, also, provide an organisation – very useful in some cases – with a source of trained teachers.

It must be said that nearly all trainees who do such courses find the experience exciting and exhausting, and you frequently hear such comments as "I've learnt more in the last five weeks than I did in my whole three years at teacher-training college . . . "

What tends to be forgotten, however – perhaps because of time – is everything which isn't language and everything which isn't methodology: in particular the learner as a learning person (dare we say such a thing?) and learning as something which isn't just a predetermined process but also (again, dare we say it?) something natural, unpredictable, and very individual.

How often on such courses is there really space, time, and encouragement for a trainee to think the following sorts of thoughts? What ability does every individual in the group in front of me really have? What are their talents? Their emotional blocks? Their emotional and mental needs? What do they think and feel towards each other? What are their human strengths? What do they think of me and how they're being taught? How do they prefer to learn English? How are they affected when their view of how they ought to be taught differs from how I, the teacher, prefer to teach them? What are the complex relationships between the individual personalities within the group they are forced to work in and what is the effect of *that* on how they, the students, learn language? What is really involved when a teacher from a different country (as is often the case) tries to teach his or her language to people from the other side of the world – not just in linguistic terms – but in terms of "students" being complex individuals who are, and have been all their lives, in many profound senses, "foreign"?

Such questions are raised from time to time but all too often they surface under such headings as "humanistic approaches" (which marginalises them) and "cultural influence" (which generalises and simplifies them). Shouldn't they be seen as a normal part of teaching?

True, trainees can reflect on their own experience of learning during the course. It helps to a certain extent, but even that is too infrequently considered for the purpose of understanding what language learners go through. The result is that trainees end up talking in ways which make it clear that they regard their students as some kind of stage army set up for them for the sole purpose of trying out their teaching skills. Fair enough up to a point, that is what they are, but unless the attitude is countered by a developing interest in the students as people, it easily becomes deep-seated and transfers itself into the "real world" when they go out there as teachers.

Another serious problem, which all trainers admit to, is the effect of pressure on the personalities of the trainees themselves. Some – probably the majority – actually like the pressure; others "crack" under it. Nevertheless, because trainers realise there is so much to be done and so little time in which to do it, many in turn treat their trainees in a less than individual way, which results in establishing the kind of attitudes just outlined. Cutting out the learner – which in effect is what it is, – even when presenting a "learner-centred methodology," is further encouraged when a trainee's own individuality and differences are implicitly made uniform by the assumption that they are all present to learn the same thing in the same way. But human beings aren't that simple and they react in different ways.

An over-concentration on current methodology[1] can also encourage cock-sure attitudes (once techniques are polished) that only later mellow into respectable self-doubt and uncertainty (on an MA course?). Besides, the methodology of mainstream ELT isn't so varied – not as varied as it likes to think it is. Certainly, it may not be organised into a single "method" but it does contain much received opinion and "techniquery" culled from many sources. This seems attractively like "a method" to trainees, no matter how adaptable it appears to experienced teachers. To a certain extent, naturally, one has to simplify on any pre-service course because there is such little time available, but too often the impression is given that even in real life things are simple and that there is a right way. Interestingly, I think it is true that most trainees don't challenge the assumptions made by such courses, at least not while they are on them. Certainly not if they want to do well. Those who do question, usually end up doing badly. I am sure this is not sinister but it is symptomatic of some of the problems thrown up by the lack of time and thinking space that usually beset such courses.

[1] The view of language presented to trainees isn't actually very varied either. Not really. It usually adheres to the current assumptions which lie behind the most recent grammar books in vogue at the time, tending to look at "items" rather than "stretches of language", and never (I think) considering language from a non-scientific point of view.

Interestingly, too, because of laws relating to the "survival of the fittest", certain teaching styles become dominant and certain personae become more acceptable than others. Inevitably teachers with a personable (i.e. helpful, amiable, and relaxed) teaching manner get by a lot more easily than those without. The old view that teachers had to be dynamic, dramatic, and in effect "show off" has more or less passed away. But, nevertheless, the teacher who can't project a pleasant personality in such a pressurised situation is quickly made to feel less confident by both the students and the trainers, and I suspect it takes them a long time to recover from this. Trainees who conform to the particular house style of the school running the course seem to survive better than those who don't – and since, in the UK at least, most house styles are similar, does this not produce a uniform brand of EFL teacher?

A further problem is that a combination of pressure and over-focus on methodology tend to create an attitude which encourages trainees to worry more about their lesson plans and their methods than they do about what (i.e. the language) and who (i.e. the students) they are teaching. Paradoxically such a presumption frequently inhibits the trainees from adequately preparing lessons and, when they teach, from having the confidence to stop worrying about the plan they have in front of them!

Lastly, every trainer knows that good trainees are those who are able to absorb criticism from others and are able to criticise themselves in a positive spirit in order to make improvements next time round. Trainees who take criticism defensively and see it as a sign of personal attack don't progress in terms of the course at all. Yet how self-critical are the trainers themselves? Yes, they will examine and criticise the organisation and mechanics of a course, but is there very much radical questioning of the basic assumptions which lie behind it?

Enough of this grumbling ... I hear my colleagues rising in resentful and probably justified complaint. Let me confess. I have run many short intensive pre-service courses and have been guilty of all the things I've just complained about. And, as I'm not alone in most of these worries, many modifications – if not radical changes – have been made. What then, within the existing framework, are the features that should be regarded as necessary in any pre-service course in addition to those that everyone agrees about?

I suggest:

1. Time must be found for trainees to involve themselves with students – to get to know them, find out about what it's like where they come

from, ask them what they think of the sort of classes they have, what they want to do, how they like to work, what sort of difficulties they have, what they think of working with each other. And so on. Activities should also be used which involve trainees in working with students rather than teaching them in the conventional way. Perhaps going over an entrance test, looking through their homework with them. Apart from anything else such involvement helps reduce the self-consciousness and nervousness trainees feel when they have to get up and "teach". They then know who they're teaching . . .

2. There should be as much contact as possible with real teaching situations, which means at the very least a lot of observation of real classes, but better still working with real classes, perhaps as an apprentice or an assistant to the class teacher. Wider use of video classes might help in achieving greater contact.

3. Trainees need to be allowed to develop their own individual teaching styles and to develop insights into the strengths and weaknesses of their own styles and approaches.

4. Calm, space, and time need to be built in to minimise neurotic anxiety and to allow trainers to give maximum support to trainees and deal with their individual preoccupations.

5. Practice lessons need to be prepared by the trainees according to their perception of "student needs" with the encouragement, support and criticism of the trainers. Decisions should be based on the students in front of them.

6. Language should be seen with more flexibility and more widely – "cut-and-dried" answers being recognised as only provisional shorthand for the "elementary" language learner. What gives a language life – in literature, for example – should also be given attention as well as the usual "linguistic analysis". At the very least language should be seen in the context of discourse.

7. Language, students, and teachers ought to be the primary focuses; methodology ought to be secondary. At the moment, on most courses, methodology is regarded, at least implicitly, as the most important thing, but can we consider the possibility of a completely different type of pre-service course? One that would work *out* from the trainees, students, and the language they are learning, rather than the usual pattern of working *in* from the syllabus, the course, the trainer, and the institution. Here are two – as far as I know – untried possibilities.

1. A group of volunteer students and a group of trainees would

produce separate sets of objectives. The trainers would then agree on/modify/reject/add to the trainees' objectives. The trainees would do the same with those of their students. Of course those of the trainers will be expressed as "learning how to teach" aims; of the students will be expressed as "improving my English" aims. The course itself then would consist primarily of the trainees working with the students with "add-on" time to look at resources, ask trainers for advice, and see classes in action or videos of classes. They could also request handouts and even lectures or seminars on particular topics that they felt were necessary. The trainer's role would be to help trainees who "got stuck" and to monitor their progress.

2. A group of trainees might work within a school as assistants to the established teachers (this already happens in one centre). The rest of the course would be in an entirely self-access mode with language-awareness tasks, videos of classes, classrooms and materials available to view. The trainees would be made responsible for organising groups of volunteer students to teach with some administrative assistance. The trainer's role would be to give periodic tutorials to review assignments and possibly to observe a sampling of lessons and comment on them. It would be important that most lessons were not observed.

These suggestions would of course present many practical problems. I am sure that many trainers, if they had a mind to, could suggest equally radical and interesting proposals. I am concerned to get the ball rolling, to start questioning the mould, and to encourage teacher-training centres to experiment with new types of pre-service course. At present we are in danger of getting stuck in a syllabus-dominated rut.

4 Martin Parrott considers the particular problems of diverse – and even conflicting – needs on short, refresher courses for teachers whose first language is not English.

Most teachers of English in the world do not speak English as their first language, and very often they teach monolingual groups whose language they share. In certain respects, there are distinct advantages to this situation. Because they themselves have learnt English, they usually have a wider knowledge of the language, especially the grammar, and a sharper appreciation of the difficulties facing their monolingual groups than their native-speaker colleagues.

Teachers whose first language is not English do however sometimes feel themselves cut off from the living language and also sometimes feel not close enough to the heart of "new ideas and new developments", although insecurity about language and methodology sometimes leads teachers into attaching undue importance to so-called "new developments". For these reasons, short, "keeping-in-touch" programmes for teachers whose first language is not English are very important: they help to provide "reality checks" for teachers and to get aspects of teaching and learning into perspective.

These are the issues which Martin Parrott deals with. Not considered in this connection is the question of initial training courses for those whose first language is not English. This however was the first type of course for overseas teachers which International House ran. Given the difficulties encountered in many countries in providing teachers with practical training, this course has played an important role in the training opportunities for teachers whose first language is not English.

Dealing with Disparate Needs on Training Courses for Teachers whose First Language is not English

MARTIN PARROTT

Introduction

This article considers short, intensive courses for overseas teachers of English, intended for experienced teachers. There is no teaching practice and the precise nature of the course is determined by the needs and objectives of the teachers who attend.

Section 1 deals with some of the problems inherent in such courses and Section 2 with ways in which the problems may be minimised or resolved. Section 3 deals with further aspects of course-planning and management relating these specifically to the qualities required of tutors running the courses.

The problems

Identifying needs and objectives

Although a certain amount of reliable information about individual areas of interest can be obtained from a pre-course questionnaire and written task, even the most comprehensive of tasks is only partially adequate. Considerable ambiguity is inevitable. However carefully the terminology is chosen, words – and the problem is compounded in a language not one's own – mean different things to different people.

Secondly, when presented with a list of options, people are inclined to choose more items than they might have chosen if no option had been presented. The converse is also true – that if areas of interest are elicited without any specific guidance, people find it difficult to know where to begin.

Thirdly, if the pre-course questionnaire or task is seen to be a component of the selection procedure, as it may well be, applicants may feel that they have a vested interest in presenting a particular "view" of themselves.

Some applicants may have only a hazy notion of what their specific needs and objectives are, while others may have a more precise idea but will modify this once the course is under way.

Not only is there a problem of identifying objectives, but once they have been identified, there is a further difficulty of reconciling disparate or conflicting objectives within the group. Factors which may affect the objectives of particular course participants can be grouped under three headings:

(a) Teaching situation
(b) Experience of learning English and previous teacher training
(c) Personal reasons for attending the course

(a) Teaching situation

A group may comprise teachers of young children as well as teachers of adolescents and adults. They may teach in the relatively privileged circumstances of a small, well-equipped language school, or may be starved of materials and resources. The groups they teach may be large or small, carefully graded or of mixed ability. They may have a heavy or light teaching schedule, their learners may be motivated or otherwise; they may attend intensive courses or may study English for only an hour or two each week. Some may teach English for very specific purposes. They may have complete freedom with regard to course design, methodology, and use of resources, or they may be obliged to adhere rigidly to a syllabus, to use particular sets of materials and to prepare students for a particular examination. The constraints they work under may be more or less realistic in relation to the needs and objectives of their students.

The circumstances in which course participants teach will clearly influence what they hope to achieve through attending the course. They may seek specific help in dealing with, for example, young children, unmotivated adolescents, particular kinds of material, mixed ability groups. Or they may be interested in the use of computers or video in language teaching, and may be impatient of too great a degree of compromise or concentration on "general issues". Very often, teachers who attend courses seeking solutions for particular problems are bound to be disappointed: they may be seeking pedagogic solutions to problems which are essentially institutional (size of courses, etc).

(b) Experience of learning English and previous teacher training

But there are also more general differences of interest, often determined by the participants' previous learning experience.

At one end of the spectrum are the teachers who look to the course to provide them with a formal framework ("I want to learn the best 'method' of teaching English"). Often these people have had no pedagogic training at all, and in extreme cases, through having learnt English outside any formal educational system (for example as a result of residence in English-speaking countries), they may even lack the conscious models of teaching that are normally obtained through the experience of being a classroom language learner.

At the other extreme are the teachers who have experienced dogmatic training in a particular method or in the exploitation of particular kinds of material. These teachers are likely to look to the course to introduce them to alternative approaches and to provide them with a framework of principle and theory, enabling them to evaluate such approaches. They do not want to be presented with a "method".

The majority, however, will probably have studied some nominal methodology already, often as one component in the final year of a degree course in English Language and Literature. People in this category commonly make one of two complaints about their pedagogic training: either that it has been too theoretical and too abstract to be related easily to classroom practice, or that it has been simply inappropriate to their teaching circumstances.

It is worth noting that, increasingly, particularly in the developing world, teachers are exposed in their training to the principles underlying the "communicative approach". However, they are unable to implement a "communicative methodology" in the classroom because of constraints of syllabus, resources, and learner expectations. Such teachers often attend the course seeking practical guidance in applying the theory they have studied or in utilising the materials they have in a way which depends neither on sophisticated technology nor on idealised groups of homogeneous motivated learners.

(c) Personal reasons for attending the course

Even when course participants teach in similar circumstances and have a common learning background their reasons for attending the course may differ and this may affect the way in which they want to study and the content of the course itself. To illustrate this, I shall sketch five profiles using common, multinational European names. (It is not my intention to suggest that any of these characteristics are related to any particular national groups.)

Rosa – Rosa wanted a holiday in the UK and decided that attending a course would justify the expense. She wants an easy time, does not want to be challenged but simply to experience being in an English-speaking environment.

Olga – Olga never enjoyed learning so much as during the year of her postgraduate teaching diploma when she was permanently "high" on a buzz of intellectual excitement. She is hoping to recapture that in an environment of stimulating and controversial discussion. Unlike Rosa, she wants both to challenge and to be challenged. She has read *all* the books and has little patience with those who have not.

Manuel – Manuel has recently been promoted to the inspectorate of English teachers in his country and feels threatened by the fact that the younger teachers, while expecting direction from him, seem to be much clearer than he is both about their objectives and about how to achieve them.

Clara – Clara began teaching about a year ago and finds that nothing she studied actually works in her classes of sixty pupils working through a rigidly controlled syllabus which is orientated towards unrealistic examinations. She has discipline problems and her confidence has been shattered. She is hoping for "magic solutions".

Max – Max is in a rut. He is a capable and confident teacher who is getting bored with teaching in a way which he now perceives as being a matter of going through the motions. He is hoping to come away from the course with renewed enthusiasm and a lot of new practical ideas.

Lack of common assumptions about learning and teaching

Partly according to age, but more particularly according to the educational traditions in the different countries from which course participants come, there may be considerable differences within any group with regard to assumptions about what learning a language involves. Assumptions are often more fundamental than just being a matter of preferring one particular teaching methodology to another.

In many parts of the world it is taken for granted that the aim of learning a language is the ability to communicate and that in any learning process students should be actively involved and should be encouraged to take some responsibility in determining the content and nature of the course of learning. But there are also many parts of the world in which it is taken for granted that the learners should take a passive role in the learning process, merely trying to absorb the language that the teacher chooses to impart. Rather than aiming at communicative ability, language education may have a very narrow instrumental or vocational function, or may even be seen as no more than an intellectual discipline, valid in itself without reference to any practical uses to which it might be put.

Before any productive learning can take place in a group within which such conflicting assumptions are represented, it is clearly necessary to bring these differences into the open and to establish a common framework of assumptions in which to plan the course.

The potential for tension and conflict

When a group of people come together for a short time to work intensively, it is obviously crucial that a positive dynamic is quickly established. In this kind of course a number of factors can work against this happening:

(a)   Age and professional seniority
(b)   Level of English
(c)   Different objectives and different backgrounds

(a) Age and seniority

For reasons of age and professional status, and depending on how these factors are viewed in a particular culture, within a group there will be those who tend to feel superior/inferior and extensively experienced/nervously inhibited – attitudes which will affect how the group determines the direction of the course. Further, different cultures have different concepts of what constitutes seniority. A junior university teacher may behave condescendingly to a secondary school head of department, and vice versa. Equally, in some cases, feelings of being junior may have a very inhibiting effect on people.

(b) Level of English

Experience shows that, above a certain basic level, there is little correlation between language proficiency and teaching effectiveness. Nonetheless, teachers of a foreign language are inevitably very conscious of their command of the language they teach. They may be proud of their abilities or anxious about what they think of as their deficiencies. In any group communicating in a foreign language, awareness rapidly develops with regard to the relative linguistic strengths and weakness of different members of the group, and this colours the degree to which individuals, particularly those at the two extremes of the proficiency continuum, feel comfortable within the group. It is not uncommon to encounter the linguistically more able course participant who insists on showing off prowess by disregarding the goal of communication, and choosing to address the rest of the group using complicated and difficult language. Sometimes initially enthusiastic and talkative participants lapse increasingly into silence as they begin to think of themselves as relatively handicapped linguistically – a problem which may be exacerbated if others insist on offering unsolicited corrections and comment.

(c) Different objectives and different backgrounds

The kinds of differences which may be envisaged in the course have already been outlined above. It is clear that conflicting objectives may give rise to impatience if participants feel that their own needs are not being met.

Differing assumptions about education may also lead to tension. Teachers from, say, northern Europe, may have little hesitation in expressing their impatience with the more conservative attitudes expressed by teachers from the developing world and, at worst, may openly dismiss their opinions as unsophisticated. The others in the group may resent any assumption that the teacher's function is other than to fill empty vessels. Clearly such attitudes if strongly felt within the group can have a fragmenting effect that may even lead to open hostility.

Approaches to overcoming these problems

Identifying needs and objectives

The problem of pre-course questionnaires can be largely overcome if a questionnaire is used in the first stages of the course with the participants (see page 33). The tutor can check, and define if necessary, understanding of the terms used. Participants can complete the questionnaire individually at home and in a later session be asked to explain the choices they made.

In addition, it is often worthwhile to ask course participants to write two or three paragraphs confidentially telling the tutor of their objectives and interests. Even if the questionnaire contains space for additions by the course participants, a confidential report will often shed further light on what is written in the questionnaire and reveal other undisclosed strong interests, often prefaced by an apology ("I don't suppose anyone else would be interested in X but . . . "). Interests can sometimes only be discerned by implication.

Once the initial diagnosis of needs, objectives, and interests has been done, the tutor then has to try to reconcile diverse, or even contradictory, interests.

It will normally be made clear to participants through advance information what they can and cannot reasonably expect from the course. The tutor will focus on areas of common interest where possible. Nevertheless divergence of interest must be faced, and the tutor will have to introduce some element of individualisation – often effectively on a sub-group basis.

I now want to look at one way (brainstorming) in which the attention of the group may be focused on some issues which are seen as individual and at aspects of individualising course content.

Task distributed on first day of course, discussed briefly and filled in individually out of class

To help me in determining the final content of this course, please indicate below how important these elements are for you giving each of them a number from one to five:

1 not at all interested in this
2 not very interested
3 so-so
4 interested
5 very interested

lesson planning
syllabuses
evaluating materials
approaches to presentation of new language items
practice activities
teaching speaking skills
teaching listening skills
teaching reading skills
teaching writing skills
teaching phonology
correction
checking meaning
use of translation
theories of language
theories of learning
"humanistic" approaches
others   ....
                ....
                ....
                ....
                ....

Please add comments where appropriate

Brainstorming problems

Many participants will probably have enrolled on the course hoping for guidance in dealing with what they see as their problems in their situation. These may relate to feelings of personal inadequacy, the

characteristics of particular groups of learners, and/or to a constellation of difficulties around syllabuses, resources, and administrative
limitations.

The diagnostic tasks will have given the tutor some insight into these
problems and on that basis he/she can prepare a discussion task sheet
in which a number of the problems are listed anonymously (see page
35). In groups, course participants can discuss these, relate them to
their own experience, analyse causes, and evaluate possible solutions,
and indeed expand the list. The tutor will have to decide whether to
form sub-groups on a heterogenous or homogeneous basis – is an
individualised element sought from the beginning or is there enough
cooperative potential to work from a point of diversity of attitude?
Such a session should take place early in the course. Participants are
reassured to find that their problems are not unique, and this even helps
to reduce the preoccupation with finding "solutions" which, even if they
can be found in any absolute sense, will not be simple or straightforward
operations. Such discussion will additionally provide a useful reference
point throughout the course towards the end of a structured session
on the extent to which the course has shed light on and modified their
view of the issues identified in this early diagnostic discussion.

Individualising content

There may be clear divisions with regard to interest. Some groups may
favour a more abstract approach; others a more practical; there may
be groups concerned with particular teaching situations. Such cases
call for devising tasks and project work in sub-groups to allow these
interests to be pursued. There is no lack of resources for project work
of this kind – notably the literature on language teaching available in
journals, books, and magazines. Additionally, interviews and visits may
be arranged and classes observed.

Any institution running such courses on a regular basis will develop a
pool of materials, including activities devised by previous groups during
the course and projects presented (after work done in the field) on their
return home. Such projects can be in various media – audio, video and
written.

In most courses, however, despite the varied interests of the
participants, people will be eager to know the fruits of each other's
research and some of these may be presented orally to the group; but
participants will certainly get a sense of fulfillment from preparing a
written report on their projects, which can be distributed to others.

Lack of common assumptions about learning and teaching

During the earliest stages of such a course it is crucial to establish the extent to which course participants share or do not share experience, assumptions about learning and teaching, and knowledge of the principles on which different approaches are predicted. In many ways it is more important to get this kind of information than to learn how the participants are used to teaching, as confusion or ignorance with regard to a particular technique can be dealt with relatively simply through description or explanation, whereas confusion or ignorance at this, more fundamental level of understanding, needs to be dealt with more carefully and often in much greater depth.

Task-centred group discussion enables the tutor to act as a diagnostician, to step in to clarify terminology where this can be dealt with on the spot, and to plan remedial strategies in the form of organised sessions on particular topics or individualised reading tasks where appropriate. An example of such a task appears below.

Task

Consider these statements made by language teachers. To what extent do you agree or disagree with their points of view? Why?

1. I never get students to work together in groups. It's a waste of time and they don't speak English.

2. I don't use a tape recorder. They don't understand most of the time and even when they do understand they aren't *doing* anything.

3. I don't speak to them in English because my pronunciation isn't very good.

4. I think you should always correct mistakes. Otherwise, how can they learn what good English is?

5. I would love to teach them to *speak* English but they have to take a written examination so I only do grammar and composition.

6. It's impossible to teach groups with students of different ability in them. I have to pretend the slow ones aren't there.

Such tasks are easy to devise and may be adapted according to the tutor's expectations with regard to the preoccupations and level of intellectual sophistication of the course participants. Where something is known of the backgrounds of participants in a very heterogeneous course, the group may be subdivided accordingly and a different task given to each sub-group.

Such activities serve also to provide course participants with the opportunity to speak personally and to listen to each other, and to initiate the process of interaction which will lead to the formation of a group dynamic. It quickly becomes apparent who is out on a limb in any way, and the tutor is able to begin planning not only areas of general content but also who should be given a structured opportunity to present to the others an individual point of view.

By such means can a tutor establish a "common language" for the course, but it cannot be expected (nor is it desirable) that these differences can be overcome during the course. Unfortunately, lack of shared assumptions is frequently accompanied by lack of tolerance.

Potential levels of tension

Although the course participants themselves are largely responsible for the extent to which the group establishes a positive dynamic, the tutor also plays an important role as catalyst.

The tutor needs to have some knowledge of the cultures and educational systems from which course participants come and to know something of their attitudes to age and status within the educational hierarchy. In this way he/she can predict potential sources of conflict and intervene in discussion to ensure that "face is not lost". The tutor may also choose to devote time early in the course to specific discussion of the roles and status of teachers in the different cultures represented as a way of encouraging participants to make clear to each other how they are seen and how they see themselves within their own educational hierarchy.

In dealing with impatience and intolerance about different educational values, the tutor must give a clear lead in showing respect for diversity of attitude. He/she must avoid any suggestion of surprise. If, as happens, he/she is called upon to defend his/her own approach to training, this should be done with particular circumspection, avoiding the danger of criticising by implication the assumptions held by those who have challenged him/her.

In approaching problems stemming from different levels of language proficiency within the group, the tutor may find it useful to discuss (early in the course) the relationship between language proficiency and teaching skills and to relate discussion of the responsibilities of learners in a mixed ability learning situation to the teacher-training course itself. Where difficulties in language proficiency reflect the first languages of the participants, the tutor can ensure that the whole group is aware of how much easier it is for a European to learn English than for an Asian. One way of doing this is to create provision in the course for teachers to teach aspects of their own languages to the group. Although the primary aim of this may be demonstration of some aspect of pedagogy, the point is quickly made to native speakers of Spanish, Swedish, or German, say, that the learning of a language unrelated to the target language is immensely more difficult. In these ways tension can be reduced. Opportunities for individual tutorials also need to be provided.

Qualities and skills required of the tutor

A tutor working on this kind of course, with its relatively imprecise syllabus, needs greater sensitivity and flexibility combined with knowledge and experience. This experience needs to be wide: the tutor who has experience in only one country, or only in private institutions, or only in teaching adults, will be hard-pressed to respond to the range of experience among the participants in the group.

Sensitivity is a quality which is required in any teacher, but in this training context, the tutor needs to be sensitive not only to the feelings and personalities of the participants, but also sensitive in responding to all the factors discussed above which often operate at a level below the surface interaction. The most important quality of all is probably flexibility. Many decisions relating to the course programme and the methodology the tutor employs can be taken only at the last moment, and still may need to be modified according to ongoing feedback.

Flexibility in course design

In short courses of this kind, the tutor faces the problem of what to leave out. It is essential that early in the course a range of options is presented to the course participants, who then provide their own additions to the list. Although some sequence of priorities can then be formulated on this basis, responsibility for the final programme is probably best left to the tutor. Even after ten hours of a thirty hour course it is difficult to draw up a definitive, detailed programme, since priorities may change as the course develops. Most tutors prefer to distribute a skeleton programme for the first week on the first day, and after six or nine hours to produce both a revised skeleton programme for the whole course and a detailed programme for the first part of it. The programme for the second half of the course can be devised just before it starts.

Participants need to be aware that any programme devised is provisional and may change according to subsequently perceived needs. The programme should contain blank spaces to allow for additional content areas to be included or simply for catching up since, however well-planned a course may be, sessions often cover only a part of the ground envisaged. It is also worthwhile programming time for feedback from course participants and in this sense the content can be negotiated. A course is organic and the ranking of priorities changes as participants respond to its content and emphases. Regular, brief sessions in which small groups discuss possibilities of condensing, eliminating and identifying anticipated topics are invaluable in allowing the "organism" to grow and evolve.

An approach such as this is not, of course, without its drawbacks. Primary among these is the pressure put on the tutor to include more and more in the course. The tutor needs to be aware of the danger of content expanding so much that there is too little time to explore profitably any of the components of the course. (A specimen negotiated programme appears on page 40.)

Flexibility of course methodology

Most participants will have some preferences about course content, but they are less likely to be sufficiently familiar with the range of teacher-training methodologies to have formed views on the ways in which their learning should be organised. Although preferences may subsequently develop, discussion of this aspect of the course in the very early stages may prove unproductive.

One approach to this problem is for the trainer consciously to employ a wide range of training methodologies in the early stages, and to focus a certain amount of discussion on the methodology itself. In any group there will be a degree of diversity in the preferences of its members. However, there are often also significant differences in preference between different groups. Some groups may favour more learner-centred approaches – activities designed to promote exchange of ideas and experience, based on brainstorming, discussion tasks, guided research, and reading. Other groups prefer lectures or demonstrations from the tutor (or from other group members), or discussion based on elicitation by the tutor. "Input" may be of particular importance to one group, while another is more concerned with process learning.

Again, attitudes towards methodology are likely to evolve and change during the course, and it may be useful to reconsider this question with participants at the mid-way stage.

Any discussion of the methodology the tutor employs can serve a dual function, as parallels can always be drawn between the teacher-training environment and the language classroom itself: through analysing their own preferences, participants can be encouraged to consider the preferences of their learners.

Flexibility in approaching individual course sessions

It is a basic tenet of all education that people learn little from exposure to ideas which are alien to their experience and existing frameworks of knowledge. They learn best when exposed to material which is largely familiar but which, at the same time, extends their thinking and knowledge.

It is particularly difficult for a tutor to gauge precisely the level of knowledge of individuals, let alone to know how to pitch "input" at an optimum level for a group as a whole. Nonetheless, "pitching" is not purely hit and miss, and in order to minimise the risks of bewilderment and boredom, the tutor needs to approach particular topics by attempting to assess the degree to which participants are familiar with the subject and the sophistication of their thinking about it. Again, brainstorming the topic, either by asking participants to list the sub-headings they would expect to use in making notes or by presenting them with a discussion task will be useful. On occasion what this leads to will necessitate a radical readjustment to the intended approach and content on the part of the tutor, but it both "warms" the participants to the subject and allows the tutor to identify who in the group can be called upon to offer a greater degree of input, and who may require particular support.

Conclusion

Many courses are run for overseas teachers of English in which a predetermined programme is followed and into which participants adapt themselves as well as they can. As will be clear from the foregoing discussion, there are numerous difficulties inherent in running courses in which an attempt is made to adapt the course to the participants. Not least among these difficulties are the demands made on the tutor, and indeed the demands made on the institution to provide tutors who have the confidence and skills required.

The success of these courses, however, speaks for itself. Not only do course participants (secure in the knowledge that no two classes are the same) return in subsequent years for courses nominally of the same kind, but tutors are also happy to run them: the rewards in terms of the scope for creativity and ingenuity happily seem to outweigh the pressures involved.

Appendix

This comprises a provisional programme issued to three different methodology/refresher courses over two years, as well as subsequent modifications to the programme (different in each case)

Provisional programme – week 1

Monday

Introductions – names, backgrounds, etc.
Introduction to the course
Discussion of objectives (see page 27)
Discussion of attitudes to teaching (see pages 28/9)
Homework: to write about teaching circumstances and expectations from the course

Tuesday

Problem-airing session
   (small groups ◊ plenary)
Accuracy and fluency
   (listening and discussion: recorded discussion of teachers with differing viewpoints)

Wednesday

What does learning a language involve?
   (discussion based on pre-set jigsaw reading tasks)
Recent changes in teaching
   (brainstorm, lecture and discussion)

Thursday

Roles and status of teachers
   (small-group discussion + reading of article from TES* ◊ discussion and vocabulary extension)
Principles of lesson planning and exploiting materials
   (elicited presentation and workshop)

Friday

To be determined

*TES = Times Educational Supplement

Course A: revised provisional programme, week 1 (issued on the Wednesday of week 1)

Thursday

Principles of lesson planning and exploiting materials
Communication and language (extension of first session on Wednesday: task-directed analysis and discussion)

Friday

Language analysis: basic procedure (workshop)
Communication activities (demonstration)
Feedback on the week and planning of second week.

Course A: provisional programme for week 2 (issued on the Monday of week 2)

Monday

Phonology warmer (demonstration and discussion)
Presentation and practice: approaches and materials (demonstration, discussion and workshop)

Tuesday

Phonology warmer (demonstration and discussion)
Comprehension skills and exploitation of materials (demonstration, lecture and workshop)

Wednesday

Phonology warmer (Maria-Angeles)
Teaching large classes (Farid)
Use of the first language in the classroom (Marie-France)

Thursday

Demonstration and discussion of: Silent Way (Soumaya); Community Language Learning (Ahmad Khadija); Total Physical Response (Kurt).

Friday

To be determined[1] (Course evaluation)

---

[1] On Thursday the group decided to use this time to review their "problems" and to present to each other materials they had come across and particularly liked.

Course B: revised provisional programme, week 1 (issued on the
Wednesday of week 1)

Thursday
Activities for oral practice of grammar (demonstration)
More on teaching grammar in a functional approach
    (lecture, demonstration and discussion)

Friday
Teaching phonology
    (demonstration and discussion)
Brief discussion of next week

Course B: provisional programme for week 2 (issued on the Monday
of week 2)

Monday
Discipline, motivation and the "good learner"
    (jigsaw reading and task-based discussion)
Open question and answer session.

Tuesday
Discourse analysis and relevance to learning and teaching
    (feedback on tasks and reading)

Wednesday
Theories of language learning
    (reading-based discussion)
Evaluation of Krashen
    (lecture and discussion)

Thursday
Teaching writing skills and correction of written work
    (lecture, demonstration and workshop)

Friday
To be determined[1]
Course evaluation

---

[1]On Thursday the group voted to use this time to have a workshop on lesson
planning using materials that some of them had brought with them.

Course C: revised provisional programme, week 1 (issued on the
            Thursday of week 1)

Thursday

Grammar workshop:
  modal verbs
  phrasal verbs
  countable and uncountable nouns
Review of materials for practising grammar

Friday

Use of video playback in ELT
  (demonstration and discussion)

Course C: provisional programme for week 2 (issued on the Monday
            of week 2)

Monday

Filming classes: use of the video camera
  (discussion based on weekend reading, practical workshop)

Tuesday

Use of computers in ELT
  (lecture by one of the course participants, "hands on" practice

Wednesday

Diagnosing errors and planning remedial work
  (analysis of tapes, discussion)
Correcting written work
  (workshop)

Thursday & Friday

To be determined[1]

[1]On the first day of the course a number of participants had expressed an interest in visiting a local comprehensive school. On Thursday most of the course visited a school and observed French classes and interviewed teachers and pupils (two course participants chose, instead, to take part as learners in advanced classes in the school and devised their own observation tasks in advance).

The first part of Friday was taken up with feedback on the previous day. One of the course participants then demonstrated how he taught songs. The group chose not to have a formal evaluation of their two weeks.

5

Ágota Ruzsa, a Hungarian teacher of English, offers us a highly personal, deeply felt reflection on the experience of the process of becoming a teacher and on the relations between teachers like herself, whose first language is not English, and native-speaker teacher trainers in TEFL. Her perspective is humanist and holistic. She writes very specifically, as both student and teacher, of her Hungarian context, but her insights are applicable to many teachers in many countries, who teach English as a foreign language. She is above all concerned with the centrality of experiencing in the learning/teaching process, and extends this criterion to teacher training.

Ágota Ruzsa tells us very clearly what teachers of English want from native-speaker trainers. Primarily, they want opportunities to develop their confidence and ability in the language (see Martin Parrott on "Dealing with Disparate Needs" on page 31); they do not want inappropriate methodologies imposed upon them. Now, of course, virtually all teacher trainers and educators would claim that they take such an attitude in any case. But we cannot be too vigilant about our hidden and unconscious motivations and aspirations in this area. Just as teachers often claim to be "learner-centred", they are so in their own terms rather than the learners' because they consistently refuse to meet the learners' expectations of what learning should be or frustrate them by withholding certain information (usually grammatical), because they "know better". Equally trainers and educators inevitably have strong internal models of what a teacher should be and do, and all too easily fail to take into account sufficiently the pedagogic world view of the teachers they are working with. Teachers of all kinds find it very difficult to avoid knowing best.

Ágota Ruzsa tells us, too, of the powerful and formative influence that the personality and attitudes of her grammar school English teacher had on her as a student of English and a future teacher. What is so striking is her depiction of her teacher's commitment to the language and her students. She worked virtually without technological facilities and yet achieved remarkable success. In effect, the only success that matters: her students came to know and love the English language. The cult of the "personality" teacher is out of favour in these learner-centred times (but as suggested above this is often set up entirely in terms of what the teacher understands by "learner-centred"!), but it may be the teacher's own relationship to the language and the rapport – in the widest sense – with the class which are the determining factors.

Such direct speaking from the heart as Ágota Ruzsa's behoves the native-speaker world of TEFL teacher education and development to listen.

Teaching from the Heart: a Hungarian Teacher's Reflections on Aspects of Teacher Training

ÁGOTA RUZSA

I have been thinking a lot about what I heard from an English friend of mine, who taught English for two years in Hungary. She says Hungary is a country of intense energy, which very often "wears out" native-speaker TEFL teachers who leave in the end, squeezed, like oranges, of all juice. She says that on a recent visit back to Hungary, she could see the effect – the weariness – on her former colleagues who have been there for more than a year.

Well, it was very surprising and fascinating for me to hear all that, since I am a Hungarian teacher of English, who lives there. What could be the reason? I kept asking myself. Are we so dangerous? Is it the "Eastern Block" effect – as might be said – of the political system? No! that would be a cheap and simplistic answer. Then I realised that I have another friend who has actually learnt the language – however difficult it is said to be – and takes a real interest in the history and culture, past and present, not to make use of it for references in future articles – but because of sheer, honest interest in another culture. *She* is not worn out!

Some other examples of TEFL teachers flashed across my mind – one, it seemed to me, came on a religious, missionary errand, thinking that we are all living in religious ignorance and in great need of conversion – and then went back disillusioned. Another came on a more liberal mission – to teach us democracy, liberalism, efficiency and real human communication – but got deterred. Another sees sensational news in every event, which might do for a nice piece at home in a magazine. There are yet other teachers who don't want anything at all to do with the country. They teach and live in their isolated expatriate circles. So what is the problem? I ask myself. A modern means of colonisation through the linguistic predominance of English? No wonder these people feel exhausted, drained, worn out – they come to "conquer", not to learn. Their minds are preoccupied, often terribly prejudiced, and not really open to the unconditional reality of a different experience. Their roots are not our roots – living under such circumstances in a country must be a draining experience.

From a pedagogic point of view it seems first to be an effort at gradual infiltration, then organised takeover – through demonstration lessons, methodology seminars and workshops. I can't help detecting a definite sense of superiority on their part. But of course like all others, this coin has its reverse side.

We, Hungarian teachers of EFL, have imposed our false, absurdly high expectations on these expatriate teachers. They may think they come as missionaries, but we welcome them as the only messengers of some real truth, who will bring the panacea for all our pedagogic headaches. We have very high expectations of them – high expectations of their knowledge of their mother tongue, their expertise in teaching methods and approaches. We are all the more pleased if they can live up to the image we carry within ourselves of the typical English person. All these unrealistic expectations stem from a lack of national identity, lack of self-confidence, and a sinister attitude of self-put-down. The real reasons, of course, go back deep into history on both sides.

So, on one hand, I find in these native-speaker teachers of English a sophisticated, refined feeling of superiority expressed through linguistic and cultural colonialism; a lack of flexibility, of empathy for other cultures, thinking, and ways of life. On the other hand, we Hungarians like so many other nations absorbed in learning how to teach English from the British, have a "blind", over-enthusiastic, anglophile attitude accompanied by low self-esteem about our place and identity in the world of teaching English.

Language is a very powerful, even magical, instrument for expressing so many visible and invisible purposes. It is also very much an expression of our sense of identity and self-esteem – it is not by accident that we speak of the "mother-tongue" – language, in a sense, like our country, gives us identity. Peoples who have been invaded and conquered and colonised are particularly sensitive to those feelings. Herder said of the Hungarians that as a people "they would sink into the Slav ocean" – but they didn't and they managed to maintain their identity by creatively reviving their language.

In the nineteen fifties – at the dawn of the new political era in Hungary – teachers of western languages such as English, French, and Italian were viewed with great suspicion and advised to take up Russian or Chinese. Russian was introduced as the first, second language in schools and became compulsory, but by no means all teachers were committed enthusiasts to the teaching of this – in itself beautiful – language. What is remarkable is that very often German or English in addition to Russian was taught by the same teacher using more or less the same methods, yet the results were surprisingly different primarily,

I believe, because the dynamic between teacher and students was also fundamentally different. I am deeply convinced that the reasons for such different results lie in the degree of personal commitment to the language taught that the teacher feels and that such an attitude crucially changes the dynamic in the group. The teaching of French is said to be not very effective in Britain – the country which is supposed to be the cradle of effective language teaching methodology; or at least which over-anxious "foreign" language teachers like myself have been persuaded by native-speaker teacher trainers is the cradle of how to teach a language effectively – perhaps the explanation is to be found in a similar lack of personal commitment to the language – in this case, French – being taught, and perhaps also in an ideological difficulty.

This sequence of reflections leads me to my second major point of analysis – that a strongly communicatively biased approach to language teaching, which aims at effective application of the language, has been significantly affected by the attitudes it reflects, as a result of its origins and its evolution having been in English-speaking countries, shaped by native-speaker teachers (themselves very often not at home in any language but their own), working in a natural language environment, usually, with multilingual classes. This has crucially affected methodology, approaches, and contexts for teaching. With the opening of borders and a vast improvement in mass communications, an influx of ELT methodology reached Hungary ten to fifteen years ago, first via textbooks, then through direct teaching contacts. All this has resulted in a real injection of energy to TEFL activities in the country. Of course approaches have been modified and tailored to our circumstances and needs, because very often these communicative textbooks and approaches outside the UK will be used by teachers who are at home in at least two languages and who work in a monolingual classroom setting, in an artificial, "enclosed", simulated English environment. The materials too frequently tend to preclude taking account of the specific national needs and tradition of learning. The task is to achieve a balance in taking from the materials and methodology what will be applicable and appropriate to ensure that our individual perspectives are maintained. The contents of coursebooks is in this respect crucial.

The idea of using authentic materials represents an enormous, step forward in dispelling the myth of suburban, middle-class "Mr and Mrs Brown", although current story-lines place young, attractive, successful "business people" at the forefront – an equally inappropriate "mythology" for most of the world's countries. There remains an overall British "feel" to contemporary materials, again, usually written on the assumption that they can be effectively used with all nationalities, races, and cultures. Opposing such tendencies, and whole-heartedly to be applauded are such books as Tom Hutchinson's *Project English* (No 1, OUP, 1987) which starts from the premise that, for example, a Hungarian learner may well not want to talk about the British legal system, health service, or any such institutions but will rather be interested in talking about personal experiences, Hungarian and world issues.

The real escape route from the "spell" of British-orientated materials is for teachers and trainers working in their own countries to write materials and books on a greater scale. Of course it is true that prior to the kind of contact with English-speaking cultures that we know today, there were hundreds of such home-produced books, but they tended to lack liveliness and individualism. The process of greater productivity of materials could be encouraged by much more contact between teachers in countries where English is widely learnt (i.e. country to country) in addition to the links between the British world of TEFL and the non-British. Like many teachers working in a monolingual context, I would welcome articles and texts about (in my case) Hungary because they would provide me with authentic examples of English; they increase student motivation because they will feel involved. The emphasis must be experiential.

It is worth reflecting on how and why it is possible to learn, even master, a foreign language in a "closed", isolated environment. My own teacher in the grammar school used boring, traditional schoolbooks – text followed by grammar and vocabulary exercises – and had no tapes or authentic listening materials, in fact, not even a language laboratory, let alone video or computers. One piece of recorded material I do distinctly remember was a record of extracts from Shakespeare read by Laurence Olivier. And I remember my teacher's voice, her pronunciation of English, and her open, truly whole-hearted enthusiasm for the language, by which means she was able to overcome the lack of technology. This interest, enthusiasm, and commitment involved us and ensured quality in our learning and her teaching. I never remember doing my English homework "in the break" – the commitment she won from us meant we just didn't do that. But she always achieved a proper balance. Her other subject was Hungarian, so there was a clear feeling of identity and rootedness. Three of my fourteen classmates became teachers of Hungarian and English. Teaching and learning from the heart – I can't imagine any better source of real motivation despite the claims of "magical" effectiveness that are made for videos, cassettes, computers and so on – these are all only machines. A language is a living, ever-changing organic entity which breathes the user's thoughts and feelings.

All that I have said has implications for the training and development of teachers, one or two specific aspects of which I will comment on. There are particular implications for British organisations engaging in teacher-training work overseas. They need to bear in mind that, generally, the teachers they are talking to and training have come down from universities at which they have received a thorough grounding in linguistics and the broader cultural aspects of English. What these native-speaker based organisations can most profitably help us to do is to develop our command of the language and our confidence in it. They can provide us with the necessary contact in this process of "perfecting" our ability in the language. This is the area of teacher development that we count as important – far more important than sometimes having methodological procedures almost imposed on us that are inappropriate temperamentally and in terms of learning traditions.

Of course, additionally, we need a continuous exchange of teaching ideas, but this is to be facilitated on a peer basis rather than by a one-way vertical, top-down process. The balance must be between training and facilitating – and this is crucial to successful interaction between native-speaker trainers and non-native-speaker teachers who have already developed as teachers and evolved a personal style.

Flow in both directions creates the desired, fruitful dynamics in which a fuller and more accepted understanding of difference can lead to a nurturing and challenging environment conducive to language acquisition. One in which all can be truly "nice" to each other, but not in the hypocritical way Lawrence comments on in these lines:

> "Americans and French and Germans and so on
> they're all very well,
> but they're not really nice, you know.
> They're not nice in our sense of the word, are they now?"

6

This article by Tim Lowe, former Director of the Distance Training Programme at International House presents an overview of the rationale behind the correspondence course and how it has been developed over a period of eight years. The setting up of this course has been the most innovative contribution which International House has made to teacher education in the field of EFL in the 1980s. For some considerable time John Haycraft had been aware that only a somewhat limited number of the eighty schools affiliated to International House were in a position to offer in-service training courses leading to the Royal Society of Arts Diploma (TEFLA), and therefore started to explore the possibilities of establishing a "correspondence course" which would lead to this qualification.

Although he is too modest to hint at the fact in his article, Tim Lowe was, in effect, the designer of the correspondence course and its major writer. Others contributed, but he evolved and shaped the overall plan and brought it to fruition.

Distance training as a mode is still relatively limited in the extent to which it offers training opportunities. But it has huge potential, especially in what it may offer to non-native speaker teachers who have to cope with large classes of children and who may never have the opportunity of travelling to the UK to attend a course. In such directions do the innovations of the 1990s lie.

A "Correspondence Course" for Teachers of English:

A Case History

TIM LOWE

Introduction

Correspondence courses have long been accepted as a means of providing education for people who are unable to attend face-to-face courses. The RSA Diploma Distance Training Programme, originally known as the "correspondence course", takes the development of professional teaching skills as its objective. It aims to meet the needs of teachers, with an initial TEFL qualification and a few years' experience, who are working in relative isolation, and want to develop professionally. Opportunities for native-speaker EFL teachers working outside the UK of taking further qualifications have always been fairly limited, because the only centres which offered training courses were in Britain or in a few city locations round the world in which courses were run by a local institution. This course was set up to provide a development opportunity for such teachers that would be as flexible as possible.

In the eight years since its inception, about 330 British, Irish, Commonwealth and U.S. teachers have followed the course in approximately sixty locations, two working in the U.S.A., several in Latin America, a large number in Portugal, Spain, and Italy; many in Morocco, Algeria, Egypt, the Gulf; two in the Lebanon, and two in Bangladesh. In its pilot stage the course was restricted to International House and British Council schools, but it is now open to any school which can field sound candidates and an able supervisor.

The course

The objectives are:

i)   To prepare teachers suitably for both the practical and written parts of the RSA Dip. TEFLA examination.

ii) To give teachers an opportunity to examine and develop their awareness of teaching and learning, especially in areas of methodology, materials, and language analysis.

iii) To demonstrate how teaching can be effectively informed by theoretical considerations.

iv) To generate potential interest in further study.

The written element of the coursework is administered by highly qualified and experienced teacher trainers at International House, London. Practical coursework in the classroom and local seminars are run by local supervisors, usually Directors of Studies or teacher trainers, who have been approved by the RSA.

The total programme comprises three components: an orientation course, a correspondence course and a local supervision facility.

The components

(See diagram on page 52.) The orientation course, a fifty-hour face-to-face course held in the summer, is based on Unit 1 of the correspondence course. The contents of this are set out on page 52/3.

The aims of this unit are:

i)   To offer guidelines and strategies for the reading and writing skills needed for long-term study.

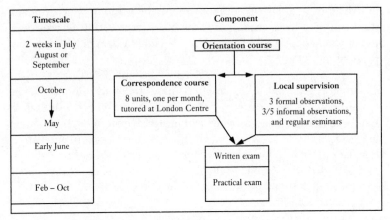

Timescale	Component
2 weeks in July August or September	Orientation course
October ↓ May	Correspondence course 8 units, one per month, tutored at London Centre Local supervision 3 formal observations, 3/5 informal observations, and regular seminars
Early June	Written exam
Feb – Oct	Practical exam

ii) To provide a broad orientation towards current issues and trends in ELT.

iii) To encourage an exchange of experiences, views, and ideas about teaching and to create a feeling of "belonging".

iv) To provide an introduction to a wide range of skills of language analysis.

v) To provide extensive observation of other teachers as a basis for the development of self-appraisal skills.

vi) To offer one to two hours' supervised teaching practice from which to establish a starting point for the practical element of the course.

Contents of Unit 1

1   A general introduction to the distance training programme

1.1 Introduction
1.2 Background to the design of the programme
1.3 An overview of the course

2   An introduction to the orientation course

2.1 Objectives
2.2 The schedule
2.3 Readings
2.4 Sample timetable
2.5 A map of the Orientation Course
2.6 A note on Unit 1
2.7 Your aims?

3   Background issues in teaching and learning

3.1 About learning and about language learning
3.2 About the teacher and about the learner
3.3 A historical perspective on methodology
3.4 Appropriate methodology
3.5 Basic terms and concepts

4 Self-appraisal skills

4.1 Changes in your teaching
4.2 An introduction to lesson analysis
4.3 Features of a "good" lesson
4.4 Developing self-appraisal skills
4.5 Informal essay assignment

5 Lesson-planning and timetabling

5.1 Introduction (lesson-planning)
5.2 The content of lesson plans
5.3 The layout of lesson plans
5.4 Your relationship to a lesson plan
5.5 Lesson-planning exercises
5.6 Introduction (timetabling)
5.7 Timetabling in practice

6 Language analysis

6.1 Introduction
6.2 First steps in analysing language
6.3 What is language?
6.4 Review exercise
6.5 Language analysis for teaching purposes
6.6 Language rules and language teaching
6.7 Phonology
6.8 Language analysis and the course material

7 Study skills

7.1 Introduction
7.2 Reading skills
7.3 Notetaking and notemaking skills
7.4 Essay writing skills
7.5 Essay assignment
7.6 Further aspects of study technique
7.7 Some "dos" and "don'ts" of approach, attitude and motivation

8 Administrative information

8.1 Information on RSA regulations, syllabus and exams
8.2 Assessment
8.3 Information we need
8.4 Reading resources for the course
8.5 Administrative reminders

The correspondence course consists of eight further units which are sent to course participants, one each month, from October to May, prior to the written examination in June. These units deal with all the topics of the RSA syllabus and cover issues of methodology, materials, language analysis, and course planning, at a fairly sophisticated level. Course participants send their written work to London, where it is marked and assessed before being returned to them. They must expect to work ten hours per week on each unit. A month's work will consist of: guided reading; self-monitored exercises; two exercises to be sent to London (often including one teaching project); one or two essays to be sent to London; and a practical teaching assignment to be assessed locally.

The titles of the eight units are:

1. Orientation, information and diagnosis
2. The introduction and controlled practice of new language
3i. Developing speaking skills
3ii. The nature of meaning; vocabulary teaching; using visual aids
4. Theoretical perspective on language and language learning
5. Developing listening and reading skills
6. Other factors affecting learning; evaluating materials and planning courses
7. Developing writing skills; error; testing
8. Miscellaneous topics (including humanistic teaching; ESP; Teaching children; etc)

In addition to this thematic structure, a section covering an area of language analysis for teaching purposes is included in each unit. Together these sections cover all major aspects of the linguistic and phonological systems of English.

Most units are accompanied by material on audio-cassette.

The role of local supervisors falls broadly into two areas:

i) Supervision of participants' practical work by sitting in on classes formally on at least four (one hour) occasions during the year. This completes the requirements of supervised teaching practice. Supervision also includes informal sitting-in as frequently as is convenient for the supervisor and the participant.

ii) As often as possible, local supervisors organise seminars and informal discussion groups for participants to provide opportunities for the exchange of ideas and experience.

Other details

i) Course participants observe other teachers for a minimum of ten hours during the course. (This includes any observation done during the orientation course.)

ii) The material includes exercises for developing self-awareness in unobserved teaching practice so that there can be effective self-monitoring and peer-observation work. One of the principal aims of the whole course is to develop the teacher's intuitive awareness to a level that will allow his/her own day-to-day teaching experience to be a source of insight, development and experiment.

The RSA Diploma practical exam is attempted by candidates between March and May and the written exam is taken in June.

Design principles

Rather than using a pre-established conceptual framework, the design of the course was the result of a process of matching overall objectives with the problems inherent in the project and with the solutions to those problems. In other words, it combined principled *ad hoc* solutions and substantial previous teacher education experience. The overriding question was: since teacher education is concerned not only with conceptual knowledge and awareness, but with the practicalities of the classroom and of creating environments conducive to learning, any distance course in teacher education must therefore address itself to this fundamental issue: given that there is to be a practical component, how is it to be realised?

Beyond this and beyond entirely normal administrative constraints on course design, issues arose that specifically related to distance. What kind of participant would be most suitable and how would this affect selection criteria? How would distance affect relationships between tutors and participants, or participants' motivation and self-reliance? How would distance affect the nature of the materials, and the content structure of the course? And how would it affect course methodology in terms of input, trainee participation, tutorial support, and assessment? What resources were needed, and what channels of communication would be most effective? How much training was necessary for the relatively inexperienced local tutoring personnel? And, finally, what kind of course evaluation procedures would be relevant and how easily could the results of evaluation be responded to?

It took four pilot years to resolve many of these questions, and others are still under continual review. Essentially, however, it is possible to refine the design features of the course to seven principal areas: a face-to-face element; personnel; material resources; content; process; course participant evaluation; course evaluation.

(i) The face-to-face element

The aim has been to replicate as far as possible the circumstances of a normal face-to-face teacher training course and this has been done by means of:

 i) 50 contact hours between participants and tutors during the orientation course.

A "mechanism model" of the programme

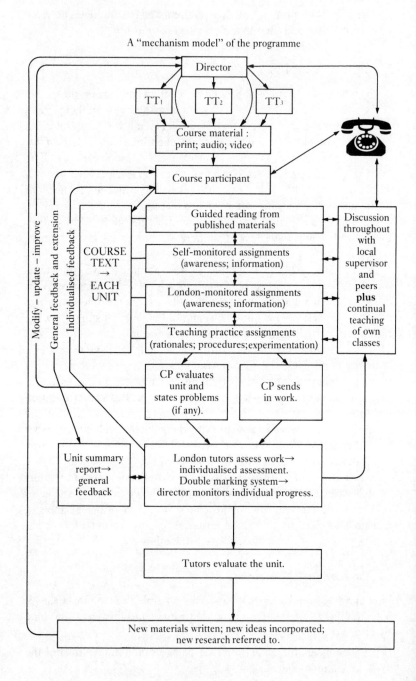

ii)   A system of local supervision through which course participants are in daily contact with senior teachers and with their colleagues in their own working environments during the year.

(ii) Personnel

Apart from the Director, the central tutoring team is made up of seven people who are very experienced teachers and teacher trainers. These tutors know what it means to cover the full range of issues that need to be included in a teacher-education programme.

Local supervisors must be experienced and qualified, too, though not perhaps to the same extent, and must have gained a good deal of experience in observing teachers, running seminars, and providing encouragement and support. Obviously, seasoned teacher-trainers working locally are automatically accepted, but Directors and Assistant Directors are given the chance to be involved also. The experience has helped several such people to become very effective teacher trainers.

The concept of local supervision is a crucial aspect of this project and a *sine qua non* of distance teacher training. In order to replicate, even in a limited way, the environment of a face-to-face course, the senior teacher *in situ* who can organise, support, clarify, help, assess, and encourage, is quite indispensable. In fact, our experience suggests that often the course in a particular local centre is significantly more successful when an exceptional local supervisor is taking part.

The partnership between local supervisors and the Director in London, together with the continual exchange of information that takes place, gets closer to the integrated training facilities of the face-to-face context.

As for the course participants themselves, basic selection criteria are that they must have previously completed a course of initial training and that they must have gained at least two years' teaching experience at a wide range of levels, preferably in more than one country. Rigorous selection criteria are important in ensuring high standards and in "weeding out" those who are unlikely to benefit from this mode of study. Applicants are further expected to have considered carefully their own suitability for self-study and the long-term commitment needed for the course.

(iii) Material resources

So far, print and audio-cassette are the primary materials used although video cassettes are already available and, given the availability of local playback facilities, these will be introduced further gradually.

Above and beyond the course material, a great deal of emphasis is placed on reading books and other materials for teachers. Adequate library facilities are essential to the success of the course.

As sources of "input", the course materials and additional published matter provide the core. But the personal and collective experience of participants and supervisors is also an important source of information and insight. Everybody is encouraged to regard what they read simply as one of several resources for the development of awareness and opinion.

(iv) Content

In principle, the content of the course is designed to meet the requirements of the RSA Diploma syllabus. In fact, it attempts to take participants well beyond this, in terms of:

  i)   A broader awareness of issues and rationales
 ii)   A more integrated conceptual framework for an understanding of the teaching/learning process
iii)   A development of many of the skills and attitudes that will benefit them in their lives generally. In this respect, it is very much a course of education rather than training.

Apart from the orientation unit (see page 52/3), the eight units of the correspondence part of the course (see above page 54), follow very approximately the traditional "order of operations" familiar to teachers. Thus, Unit 2 deals with the introduction and controlled practice of new language (i.e. issues relating to "accuracy"), Units 3, 5 and 7 deal with developing the language skills (i.e. issues relating to "fluency"), and Unit 7 deals with testing. Practical theory and terminology are introduced gradually and judiciously, with more major theoretical input at Units 3ii, 4 and 6. Issues of planning and materials exploitation are focused on in Unit 6 thereby reviewing many of the concerns of earlier units. A language analysis component runs throughout the whole course.

The content of the course is structured to achieve the following goals:

  i)   To move from what is familiar to what is less familiar.
 ii)   To move from a consideration of current practices to a consideration of theoretical perspectives which might inform or develop those practices.
iii)   To organise assignments at appropriate levels of cognitive complexity to take into account the high motivation and energy levels in the early stages of the course, and the declining levels thereafter.

iv)   To encourage participants constantly to make connections between all aspects of the language teaching/learning debate, by means of linear and cyclical currents running through a thematic landscape. A modular course, in which each unit were a separate entity, would make this impossible.

v)   To provide a "hidden curriculum" of developing themes such as: the "good" language learner, learner training, teacher self-appraisal, pragmatics in language teaching, and so on. These have come to be called "cross-themes", since they intersect with the core themes continuously throughout the course.

Each unit is structured round the following framework: participants begin by reflecting on their own current practice; they then consider relevant "theoretical" insights by means of reading, discussion, and awareness-raising exercises; and finally they explore the potential of these insights for generating new ideas for classroom practice in their own teaching.

The language sections of all the units comprise in total a pedagogically-oriented analysis of the four main language systems: grammar, lexis, phonology, and discourse. The relationship between linguistic form and communicative meaning is a continually recurring theme, and participants are expected, by the end, to have a particularly keen understanding of this issue.

In summary, the content of the programme is deliberately "practice-driven" rather than "theory-driven", so that the starting points for discussion of particular issues derive from classroom-oriented problems rather than those problems and conceptual categories identified by theoreticians.

(v) Process

The process/product debate is now regarded as one of the central concerns of educators. Rarely, however, is either of these concepts explicitly described: rather the terms are referred to loosely as needing to be somehow in balance according to the objectives of any particular learning encounter.

The process at work in and between participants and tutors are regarded as fundamental to success, and the qualities that should inform them have been carefully considered.

The process is seen as having five basic dimensions, all of which are inter-related:

–   the acquisition of knowledge and awareness

- the development of intellectual skills
- the influence of affective/attitudinal factors
- the development of pedagogic skills
- the influence of physical states and conditions

It is envisaged that knowledge and awareness will be acquired through the normal means of reflection, reading, discussion and the writing of assignments. Here, much emphasis is placed on collaborative, as opposed to individual, effort, in the belief that people absorb information better when they can talk or write about it with others – i.e. the local supervisors and other participants. The style of assessment of written work is also carefully "geared" to promote this process.

Intellectual skills, such as exercising critical judgement, identifying and solving problems, and organising one's arguments, are encouraged throughout the course, in seminars and written work, and again the style of assessment is in tune with this objective.

The affective/attitudinal dimension concerns the development of characteristics such as involvement, informed scepticism, confidence divergent thinking, originality, and so on. Foundations are laid for this aspect of process during the orientation course, and are built upon throughout by means of specific kinds of assignments, approaches to assessment, and regular seminars.

Pedagogic skills are developed, as on many part-time training courses, through the nature of the training situation itself, in that participants are able to teach their own classes during the course and are therefore able to assess how their teaching can be usefully informed by theoretical insights and new ideas. Self-appraisal, peer-appraisal and observation by supervisors blend with specified teaching assignments designed to promote experimentation and reflection.

The importance of the physical dimension is particularly highlighted in a distance-based course. Exhaustion caused by the sheer amount of work can render the best learning efforts virtually useless. Participants are therefore encouraged to leave work unfinished and move on to new material whenever the task seems insurmountable.

(vi) Evaluation of course participants

Evaluation principles have been established to fit the particular process-product rationale that has been developed for the programme. There are essentially four opportunities for evaluation of course participants: self-monitoring of informal written work by the use of a key of suggested answers contained within the course material; informal self-evaluation of practical teaching; external formal evaluation of practical teaching by local supervisors; external evaluation of formal written work by tutors in London.

By trying to create a learning experience that generates maximum participation and personal development, it has been ensured that most assignments are both low risk (i.e. they are self-monitored) and high reward (i.e. in terms of the extent of learning product and process that takes place). Such assignments are challenging and manageable, and are intended to be used mainly for awareness-raising and information gathering.

Those formal assignments required to be assessed in London tend to demand more structured, polished thinking, and to be "geared" to points in each unit at which course participants might be expected to be able to tie together several threads and produce well-formed discussions of issues.

From the orientation course onward, there is an emphasis on participants adopting both the attitudes and skills needs for self-reliance as developing teachers. One dimension of self-reliance – the ability to appraise one's own teaching – is given special prominence throughout the course through both written and practical assignments.

The pressures on participants of working at a distance require an evaluation philosophy and an affective network which are supportive. Thus, efforts are made to promote collaborative study; risk-taking and originality are rewarded as well as knowledge and good presentation; and we provide an assessment "cushion" so that the four least successful of the fourteen formal assignments are discounted in the final assessment.

In summary, there is a heavy emphasis on detailed individualised, qualitative evaluation (which is, incidentally, expensive in terms of programme running costs), a feature which makes the programme unique.

(vii) Course evaluation

During the pilot years an external moderator was appointed by the RSA, who provided most fruitful and supportive feedback. The ELDS at the British Council has also taken a keen interest and channelled useful comments back. The course participants send in end-of-unit evaluations, and a regular exchange of information with local supervisors provides another important source of feedback. In

London, tutors also regularly offer suggestions for modifications. End-of-course evaluations are requested from all and, since the course is in easily modified typewritten form, any constructive suggestions for improvements are not difficult to incorporate.

Problems

The setting up of the course was not without its problems although most of them have now been either solved or accepted as inevitable. For instance, the text, in efforts to leave nothing to chance and in trying to incorporate all the possible queries that might arise in a face-to-face context, tended at times towards overkill, so that a topic was in danger of being done to death. It was sometimes difficult to show which parts of the information were central and which peripheral to the issue in question. Instructions were difficult to make absolutely unambiguous and, above all, the fact that it was all in written form gave it too much authority in the minds of participants, which detracted from their independent thinking.

Postal delays, the slow and painstaking assessment procedures, and the periodic loss of motivation and confidence among course participants during the year are still problems, but continued thought is given to easing them. A more profound problem perhaps is that the course is not, unlike many correspondence courses, in either sense of the word, an open course. Numbers are limited and only native-speaker teachers whose level of teaching skills has already been externally validated at an initial level are admitted. Dates are fixed, again unlike many correspondence courses which can be followed with considerable flexibility in terms of time.

Results

The results of the Distance Training Programme candidates in the RSA Diploma examination have been above 80% since the course started, and since the introduction by the RSA of a system by which exam performance and course assessment are combined to form an overall result, the course has attained a 95% pass rate. This is well above the average success rate throughout the world, which hovers at around 65%. Each year several candidates achieve distinctions in either the practical or written parts of the examination; of those who re-sit, 95% invariably pass. Over seven years only seven people have dropped out.

Perhaps more important than the examination results is what has been realised for individuals in terms of broader development and self-awareness. What is more, the locally-run seminars and peer observation schemes seem regularly to draw in and stimulate other colleagues, thereby enhancing teacher development generally within the school concerned.

Conclusion

The RSA Diploma reflects the privileged educational environment of motivated adult learners in small classes. This can mean that teachers working in so privileged a context, and flushed with the rewards that come from such a context, may be significantly more motivated in a distance training course than their counterparts in educational systems in which teachers (whose first language is not English) have to cope with large classes of children. Until distance teacher-training squarely addresses itself to such areas, it cannot be said to have achieved very much. But to use the privileged training environment as a laboratory for this mode of training is, perhaps, one of the best reasons for doing it at all.

7
Phonology is probably the principal content area in training courses which intimidates trainees. They sometimes have an attitude that parallels Monsieur Jourdain's: in Molière's play he realised with surprised delight that he had been speaking prose all his life; trainees, on the other hand, are more likely to realise in appalled dismay that they have been using phonology all their lives and must now attempt to understand how it works!

Brita Haycraft argues that phonology is neglected, but must be demystified for teachers in training by reducing the technical background information at the initial training stage to a minimum and encouraging them to apply positive attitudes immediately in teaching practice.

Phonology and Initial Teacher Training

BRITA HAYCRAFT

Pronunciation, by which I mean phonology in action, is probably the least favoured subject to teach. Ask a colleague to take a "pron" class and various avoidance strategies can be observed. Even EFL coursebooks rarely contain notes on "how to say it", and if they do, they have been known to lose them in later editions, for fear of harming sales! But in real life terms, pronunciation is of great use to learners, helping them to experience the language more vividly, so making it more memorable and accelerating the learning.

Much, however, depends on how pronunciation is first presented in the classroom, in turn dependent on how it was introduced to the teacher while training. Judging by the results, the experience in many cases can't have been very positive.

If foreign language learning has improved over the last twenty years, it is probably due more to increased travel at a younger age than to changes in the classroom. True, techniques have developed in many and exciting ways, though not, it seems, for the teaching of pronunciation. Priorities are still such that, whereas teachers occasionally try to "mend broken sounds", students are often left unskilled in how to tackle the utterance as a whole. Syllabuses have no built-in progressive pronunciation training. What is the malaise?

A first teacher-training course is at present pretty daunting with regard to the phonology component. In a matter of weeks, on intensive courses, the trainees are supposed to learn not only the component systems of pronunciation, but also how to teach it. Perhaps the aim over-reaches itself and it is time for a different approach.

A different approach

Changes can be envisaged in course content, in the order of presentation and in the general attitude.

If most of the theory of intonation, rhythm, and sounds were postponed to a later course, the tutor would have time to relate essential phonology to immediate practical application in the teaching practice, and trainees would feel less overawed. The august term "phonology" could be replaced with the more down-to-earth "pronunciation help".

If moreover it became standard to work on shaping the utterance first, in the general English lesson, before attending to sounds, the learner would see the process as being of immediate, practical benefit. Learning would consist mainly of imitation with a few explanations and simple instructions, which students could act on and develop.

It is also important that all the tutors involved in training courses should share in highlighting the role and potential of pronunciation in any speaking exercise, thus establishing it as an accepted part of the general teaching process instead of relegating it to special seminars. In this way the pronunciation element would be dealt with mainly in the general preparation for teaching practice, with only four or five special seminars for further clarification and peer practice.

Teach now – learn phonology later

How far trainees will be able to give pronunciation help without much of a background in phonology is a valid question. But speaking is after all a physical activity and it might work better if the teaching were less technical and took more account of common sense. Such an approach might also appeal more to trainees.

What follows is an outline, presented step by step, in order of appearance on an initial training course, as it were, accounting for the minimum trainees must know and should be able to do, by the end.

(i) Introducing the pronunciation component

Right at the start, the course tutor introduces pronunciation in its wider function as the speaker's way of giving life to the whole utterance – in effect of speaking expressively – by various means, and relates it to the students' situation. Encouragement to use intonation makes even beginners sound expressive, as can be demonstrated with the right kind of work on any line from a coursebook dialogue. E.g. "Hello, excuse me, is this the way to the station?" "Have you got any change?" "What's the time?" By stressing this word rather than that, even beginners can project meanings without using extra words, as in "What would *you* like?". "Have *you* seen *Psycho 2?*"

By linking words and contracting unstressed grammatical words (e.g. should, did, at, for) without much meaning of their own means the students can speak faster, more smoothly and more interestingly.

E.g. "I've got a ticket," "They're sitting on a sofa," "I think it's awful".

In addition, an introduction to word stress will give confidence with longer words, such as 'confident, phi'losophy, 'secretary, repres'entative.

These are the initial speech skills to promote in the general language lesson. They are simple points that trainees can understand and give help with straight away.

After this short overview, within the context of general lesson preparation, the tutor should get the trainees to consider the pronunciation factor in the language items they individually have to teach, i.e. is there a good opportunity for practising intonation? What is the speaker's attitude? Which words should be stressed? Is the utterance too long and how can it be trimmed or divided? Any useful word-links to point out to students? Any weak forms? Any recurrent word stress pattern? Any particular sounds to work on?

Apart from familiarising the trainees with basic features of phonology and common pronunciation problems, this process also gets them to test the examples aloud, expressively. By doing so, they get useful practice in voice projection and natural delivery, and it helps them to eliminate unwieldy or stilted examples. A short demonstration by the tutor will show that this preparation can be done quite quickly.

Just as grammar and vocabulary are considered from the points of view of selection and grading, so is the pronunciation angle examined. The difference is, however, that while the grammar and vocabulary change and vary and become more complex, the basic aspects of pronunciation remain much the same.

(ii) Practice

The amount of practice students should be allowed is another point to consider with trainees. Any French or Italian conditional clause given to the trainees to practise will soon convince them just how many repetitions students will need, and clamour for, before going on to the next item. It is important to encourage plenty of lively repetition practice. Repetition need not take the form of mindless drills but can be exuberant and creative.

(iii) Praise

Another key point is appreciation. Any attempt from the students "to get it right", especially the stress positions and attempts at intonation, should be commended even if the grammar is faulty, just as a wooden delivery, however accurate, should be tried again with more life. Students must be made aware that the teacher cares about the pronunciation features.

(iv) Teaching practice

In the teaching practice feedback, the tutor makes sure of commenting on the pronunciation help given, such as the trainees' own voice projection, and appropriate style, and clear modelling leading to lively repetition. It is important to be simple and brief, avoiding excessive or irrelevant detail.

The importance of a definite process of integration cannot be over-emphasised. In addition to this integrated pronunciation work, there is of course also a need for some sessions in which a variety of pronunciation and phonology matters may be dealt with in some depth. But the first thing to get across is not to treat "pronunciation" as an end in itself, but as a means of speaking with more spontaneity and facility, leading to more initiative in conversation.

Fluency practice and letting the students try out how the utterance is said can actually lubricate the general language-learning process – although few of us were ever made to feel that, when struggling with foreign languages. The aim is to counter and by-pass common learner problems.

It may also be necessary to re-establish the reasons for working on the attitude, focus, and speechflow of the overall utterance, the correction of sounds coming a definite second. It seems extraordinary that all this time pronunciation teaching has begun with the sounds in a language which caused Tolstoy to remark "The English are funny. They write Manchester and pronounce it Liverpool". The utterance features cause far less anxiety, and if you are complimented on your good English, it is because of your handling of stress and intonation, not because of your perfect sounds.

Much of the work will merely consist of learning to give subtle, imaginative, and effective "reminders" to students. The question of how long to go on correcting one single item is worth raising, as well as how students can be encouraged to practise items at home.

Common student problems and weaknesses

Trainees will want an overview of students' difficulties. The following are the principal ones within each pronunciation area that need attention from the start.

Problems for many nationalities

Intonation: Remains flat or assumes a questioning tone out of general hesitation and uncertainty about new words. Main remedy: simply encouraging the students to express the appropriate feeling through interesting situations and materials. Also exploiting attitudes such as politeness, delight, surprise, or fury when they appear in practice dialogues.

Stress: Students tend to stress words and syllables randomly, mostly because they have never thought about it and don't on the whole get reminded about it. Main remedy: introduced from the beginning, the main stress is always pointed out and practised, with much praise, until students take to it. The use of stress as a context pointer is also constantly exercised in personal exchanges such as "What would you *like?*" "And what would *you* like?"

Word-linking: Hesitation again makes students stop and start between words. Main remedy: encouragement to say the words together and to say all the phrase a little faster. As necessary, draw a loop between words on the board, e.g. I'm‿a, in‿a, reading‿a, I'd‿like. ·

Syllable contraction of weak forms: Obviously students will feel doubtful about reducing whole words like *have* /əv/, *would* /d/ or *will* /l/ to almost nothing. Main remedy: reinforcement of surrounding stresses so as to favour contraction and saying the phrase a little faster. Clear information about the most common weak forms. Discouraging certain strong forms from the start, especially for *is, was, is not, are not, were not* as well as *can, can not.*

Word stress: All students stress long words haphazardly, as in **hos**pital, mu**si**cian, and maison**ette**. They also tend to pronounce the unstressed vowels too clearly. Main remedy: always correct wrong stress, practising ever faster repetitions to favour schwa /ə/, or indeed total syllable loss as in *interesting* /'intrəstɪŋ/ and *interested* /'intrəstɪ.d/.

The sounds: All students maltreat the specifically English sounds th /θ/, w /ɯ/, oh /əʊ/, ah /ɑː/, as well as almost totally ignoring the use of schwa /ə/. Main remedy: plenty of practice through imitation, encouragement and patience.

Schwa /ə/ is particularly well practised in long words such as *photography* /fə'tɒgrəfɪ/, probably /'prɒbəblɪ/, usually /'juːʒuəli/, while ah /ɑː/ should be pursued in the common words *ask*, *aren't* and *party*, and oh /əʊ/ chased in *no, go, so, don't, going* and *won't*. W gets practised the whole time in *was, were, when* and *where*, etc, as does th /ð, θ/ in *the, this, that*, and in *dates*. There is no need to go looking for special phrases or tongue-twisters.

Much student error results from bewilderment about spelling, especially "double" vowels like *ea, ei, ie, ou*, and *oa*; sequences like *ough*; and *w* in *law, new* or *allowed*, let alone the *-ed* ending in *opened, finished, happened* and the like. Main remedy: explaining the more troublesome letter-sound relationships, plus the use of the English alphabet sounds.

As these problems are learner-based rather than nationality-based, the same training is appropriate for all students.

Problems for some nationalities only:
Many nationalities other than speakers of Slav and Germanic languages have difficulty producing consonant clusters, especially at the end of words, as in *books, looked* and between words as in *What's that? It's difficult*. The reason Spanish speakers say "Espain" and "estrong" is that they find it hard to say "s" plus a consonant at the beginning of words and so put in a "support" vowel. Main remedy: where possible use word-linking to ease these clusters. Some students get it straight away.

Speakers of Latin languages have difficulty with the longer and shorter vowels, of which the *leave-live* example may be the most striking. Main remedy: imitation, and whenever possible comparing the pronunciation of "international" words like *minister* and *meeting*, and attempts to lengthen or shorten the sounds, never allowing "Eet eezent".

There are a number of other problems with sounds, such as voicing or aspiration, the l/r confusion, the h and the j (especially for Spanish mother-tongue speakers), as well as the /e/–/æ/ and /æ/–/ʌ/ confu-

sions. Until there is time to deal with these difficulties, it is important
not to make fun of them but to accept them as temporary flaws and
boost the students' confidence. Some of the sounds will simply right
themselves as time goes on. The simplest remedy is to let the students
hear how the teacher produces the sound. Fellow students able to offer
a model can also be encouraging.

Tutors may want to list the various points on "handouts" but should
make sure not to flood trainees with information that might alarm them
and deter them from helping the students.

More teaching ideas

There will be a demand from trainees for further teaching ideas. A
simple way is to try out various techniques in peer teaching, such as
the use of "moodcards" to trigger off a livelier voice-movement. Ask
the class if a particular student really sounded happy/sorry/angry, etc.
Use the provocative question technique: e.g. "Is Christmas in April?"
in order to obtain an expressive contradiction rather than a mere
answer.

It is useful to organise ways of exchanging personal information
in a chain, in groups or pairs, simulating conversation and moving the
stress to "you" or "your", while also practising a tense. E.g. "I went to
the cinema last night. What did *you* do?"

By scanning the dialogue for helpful word-links, trainees note how
similar consonants seem to merge, e.g. *what did, with the, locked the,
we'll look*, and how a tense may get "concealed". They can also see how
word-linking can facilitate the final *-ng, -s* or *-t*, when a vowel follows,
serving to break up consonant clusters.

As for weak forms, trainees can be led to observe how firmly
established stresses make it easier to contract the unstressed words
in between. Getting to know the phonemic script and its advantage
over the spelling convention is essential and trainees may participate
in marking the sounds "at risk" in a special colour and enter a few
differently spelt (everyday) words under each symbol together with the
bonus of phonemic script for weak forms, e.g. *we'd have* /wiːdəv/, *must
have been* /mʌstəbɪn/.

Certain correction techniques known to work without seriously
disrupting the lesson can be tried out, but it is important not to dwell
too long on correction which may undermine the students' confidence.
Difficulties should be played down. It is also useful actually to do
exercises meant for students with trainees – for example, marking the

stress in a dialogue as it is played or, better still, predicting the likely stress positions before playing the tape.

Various word-stress rules come to light through tasks such as grouping mixed vocabulary according to the stressed syllable, counting from the end. Or comparing the stress position, and the vowel sounds, in international words as pronounced in English and then in another language – a highly revealing exercise.

Rationale

The pronunciation package on initial teacher-training courses might succeed better if trainees got into action without too much prior information and a few standard instructions. The outline suggested above is considerably shorter and phonologically less ambitious than on many current training courses, but it allows good foundations to be laid. Particularly important is the order in which the main areas are presented. By turning it round, it now tallies with the speaker's reality and should work better. It makes sense to practise the entire utterance first, simply because we do not speak in single sounds but in "chunks" and stretches within which sounds interact. Children perfect the sounds long after having conversed in faulty syllables with excellent stress and intonation. If the phonemes have come to be studied first because the alphabet initiates writing, perhaps it was a false analogy, given that all manner of phonetic realisations, including weak forms, depend on the speaker's decisions about speaking speed, voice movement, and stress.

Conclusion

It is time language teaching, still firmly rooted in the written form, accepted the spoken form as at least equally important. If the pronunciation element were seen in a more practical way, and made more simple to start with, teachers, and in turn students, would take more kindly to it and developments would snowball in productive directions, eliminating myths and fears. After all pronunciation in language teaching means talking – students talking. If encouraged and guided with care, they all have the capacity to get off to a good start. This is what we should tell trainees – and get them to do.

8

Rod Bolitho reflects on the place of language analysis in the training of teachers and how to develop their linguistic awareness in order to lay solid foundations of knowledge. He considers this issue from the perspective of three different types of course – initial training (RSA Certificate), post-experience (RSA Diploma), and courses for teachers whose first language is not English.

This question is crucial in training and development of teachers, especially during a period of considerable instability about the status of grammar and how it should be dealt with both from the learner's and teacher's points of view. The teacher's attitude to this question of language is a determining factor: sometimes – more so in the case of teachers who are native speakers of English – it seems that the 'L' – language – in ELT is forgotten as teachers become absorbed with methodologies, procedures, interpersonal skills, counselling skills, and teacher development activities. Yet it is language which the language learner wishes to acquire with the help and guidance of the teacher and in achieving this aim it is fundamental that the teacher should have a deep and wide-ranging knowledge of the language being taught. Awareness must be informed by knowledge, and teacher education must aim to equip teachers with the motivation and means of acquiring this knowledge as a life-time's project. This is all the more important in our time when, as Rod Bolitho points out, many teachers and potential teachers arrive on training courses with no basis of linguistic understanding or insight derived from their general education.

A fundamental personal quality required in a teacher of a language is a genuine interest in and knowledge of that language. "Awareness" that is not sustained by knowledge is inadequate.

Language awareness on Teacher Training Courses

ROD BOLITHO

Most training courses in ELT, particularly at initial level, include a component concerned specifically with the analysis of language. The days when native-speaker status was considered sufficient guarantee of linguistic proficiency are long gone, and this language component is considered just as essential for native speakers as for those whose first language is not English.

What still varies enormously, however, is the way in which the need for language analysis is interpreted and met. There are some courses – I was on one as a trainee myself in the late sixties – in which the emphasis is on linguistics: participants are introduced to various theories of language and models of grammar and are asked to show their understanding of these in assignments or examination answers. It is often difficult for trainee teachers to see the immediate relevance of such an approach to their understandable preoccupation with survival in the classroom. On some other courses, trainees are pointed towards reference grammars which are supposed to inform their own teaching and towards pedagogic grammars such as their students might use. The encounter with both types of grammar, the reference most often descriptive these days and the pedagogic still (by popular demand!) more prescriptive in nature, can be lonely and bewildering, particularly if the language analysis component is not clearly related to the methodology component on a course. After all, trainees today are joining the profession at a time when the place of grammar in a communicative syllabus is still being worked out. Yet it is emerging ever more clearly that grammatical accuracy is still an important element in the development of communicative competence, although there are considerable differences of opinion about how this is best handled. There is a fairly widely held view that it is probably more effective to adopt an inductive, insight-based approach to grammar than to give rules and expect learners to apply them. If this is what trainees are expecting learners to do, it seems reasonable to try to build an approach based on insights and awareness-raising into training courses.

The grammatical and lexical systems make many teachers on in-service, post-experience courses tense and nervous. Teachers whose first language is not English often do not like to admit gaps in their knowledge in a public forum, yet they are naturally insecure about many aspects of the language they teach. Native speaker teachers frequently have their own tried and trusted formulae for grammar teaching, and do not take kindly to attempts to revise their views. Initial trainees need a safe framework, which will allow them to "blunder about" for a time while they put up and test their first hypotheses about the language they are to teach. Most groups of teacher trainees are 'mixed ability' groups when it comes to knowledge of language systems. Any approach to language work on a training course will therefore need to take account of:

– the teacher's prime need to be secure about the language to be taught;

- the need to get trainees to relax and discuss language problems openly;
- the need for trainees to become familiar with reference grammars and learners' grammars, and to be able to look critically at the way language is presented in coursebooks;
- the need for language work on the training course to be perceived as relevant to the demands of the classroom.

My aim is to illustrate how an "awareness-raising" approach[1] can be used to help trainees to meet these requirements on three different types of course:

(i)   initial training courses for native speakers
(ii) post-experience training courses for native speakers
(iii) in-service "refresher" courses for teachers whose first language is not English

(i) Initial Training Courses for Native Speakers

An example of this type of course is the Royal Society of Arts Certificate in the teaching of English as a Foreign Language to Adults. On such a course, time is usually at a premium and the great majority of participants have little or no prior experience of TEFL. These two factors mean that the training team will almost certainly have to take responsibility for selecting and ordering the main topics to be included in the language analysis component of the course. Many problems are predictable at this level (e.g. distinguishing between form and function, acquiring basic descriptive terminology, learning about the relationships between tense and time, and tense and aspect), and many more will derive from micro-teaching, teaching practice sessions, and early tussles with coursebooks. More and more initial trainees are arriving on courses without even a basic working knowledge of the systems of their own language and are uncomfortably surprised to find, in early classroom encounters, that some adult learners, after years of formal language study at school, know more about grammar than they do! So classroom survival becomes the main consideration; there is not time for more than initial sensitisation. A typical list of topics covered on a course at this level might include the following:

---

1   The main references here are to grammar and lexis, but the phonological system, too, is susceptible to a similar "awareness-raising" approach. See, for example, the practical exercises in Hawkins, E *Awareness of Language* (CUP) and its accompanying cassette.

Grammar terms
Form and function
Present
Past
Hypothetical meaning
Modals
Question forms
Passive
Future time
Researching grammar after the course
Tense vs aspect

Aspects of these would be taught in micro-teaching or peer-teaching sessions, and subsequently "talked about" by pairs or groups of trainees working together. A total of 12–14 hours of course time (out of a total of 100 hours – the RSA requirement) might be devoted to language analysis.

Below are two sample language awareness worksheets, which could be worked on individually or in small groups, with a subsequent plenary discussion to check perceptions and deal with problems which arise.

1. Talking about the future

> **It is important to know what a speaker
> has in mind when referring to the future**

Assign each of the following utterances to one of the categories of meaning which precede them:

A. predicting
B. stating intention
C. making an offer
D. making a request
E. a warning based on visible evidence
F. announcing a plan that has already been decided
G. stating a possibility

1) Be careful. You're going to knock that vase over!
2) Shall I open the door for you?
3) Perhaps I'll see you on Saturday.
4) I'm going to consult a solicitor before I reply to that letter.

5) Will you send that letter on to me when it arrives?
6) I'm sure you're going to enjoy working here.
7) The queen is not going to stop in the Gulf on her flight to the Far East.
8) I'll give you a hand with that suitcase.
9) It looks as though it's going to rain.
10) He's not going to find it easy to cope with being unemployed.
11) You will lock both doors, won't you?
12) There will be no tax concessions to home-owners in the budget according to informed sources within the government.
13) You'll never finish that novel by the weekend!
14) Look out! The potatoes are going to boil over!
15) Maybe she will agree to the plan now that she understands it better.

(NB This is one of a sequence of exercises on "Future Time".)

2. Form and Function

(This is to be used as a quick revision exercise, at the end of an introductory session.)

Look at the example (1), then try the exercise, making brief notes in the columns on the right.

	Form Interrogative (Yes/No question)	Function Request
1) "Can you lend me £5?"		
2) "What time does the match start?"		
3) "Be careful. The floor's wet."		
4) "Shall we go for a walk?"		
5) "You ought to take life a bit easier."		
6) "Well done! I never thought you would get the job."		
7) (confrontation between two people) "What do you think you're doing here?"		
8) (one person bursts into a room; the other comments) "Were you born in a field?"		
9) "You must be joking!"		
10) "I'd love a cup of tea."		

On an initial course, it is likely that the trainer will have to monitor perceptions carefully, and be ready to offer explanations, definitions, and interpretations, as trainees will often (in their keenness) jump too readily to wrong conclusions.

It is useful for trainees at this level to familiarise themselves with a simple learners' grammar such as *A Basic English Grammar* (Eastwood, J and Mackin, R, OUP (1982)) and to be able to see how it can be used to supplement the coursebook. By the end of the course, they must at least know where to look up grammar points when confronted with problems during lesson preparation.

(ii) Post-experience training courses for native speakers

Examples of this type of course are the RSA Diploma in TEFLA, and many courses leading to a Postgraduate Certificate or Diploma in Education. Given the post-experience nature of almost all courses of this type, the training team can contemplate a different approach to the selection and prioritisation of topics for the language analysis component of the programme. There are further reasons for this:

> trainees' experience will vary in extent, in depth, and, of course, in terms of geographical location. This means the group will be of mixed-ability, ranging from those who have worked quite closely on language to those who have "bluffed" their way through and still have not confronted the main issues;
>
> trainees need to become thoroughly familiar with a reliable reference grammar, and to develop the confidence to assess and supplement practice materials for learners;
>
> one of the most common reasons for failure or poor performance in the teaching practice component of many courses at this level remains the inability to analyse language adequately for teaching purposes;
>
> the need for much greater depth in linguistic understanding at this level.

All of this points to a need to consult fully with trainees in drawing up a list of topics, and to make the materials for language analysis available in a form which makes it possible for them to be used either collaboratively in course sessions, or individually in sessions, or even at home. In any case, the materials should be made available on a self-access basis, allowing trainees themselves, either individually or in groups, to dictate the pace at which they move.

The following procedure seems to meet most of the needs identified above:

1. "Pyramid" discussion to establish a priority list of topics. This works in the following way: individual trainees write down, in order, the three language areas which they least like teaching. They then compare notes with a partner and reduce their separate lists, by negotiation, to a priority list of three. Then, groups of four are formed, and a single list of three topics is agreed on by each group. Through the process of reflection and discussion which is involved in all of this – which may take one to two hours in all – trainees learn to work together, to compromise, and to understand problems from different points of view. Much is clarified, terms previously used loosely become more precise, and good "tips" are passed on. Finally, much reassurance is derived by trainees from talking openly about difficulties with language analysis which they experience.

2. The priority lists for each group are displayed on an overhead transparency or wall poster. A course I worked with recently established the following priorities:

	PRIORITY 1	PRIORITY 2	PRIORITY 3
Group 1	Present perfect Simple/ Continuous	Articles	Infinitive/Gerund
Group 2	Modals: Didn't need to/ needn't have; must, dare, ought to, etc	Future Time	Defining/ Non-defining relative clauses
Group 3	Gerunds vs Infinitives	Articles (presentation)	wish/would & did/had
Group 4	Sentence and phrase structure	Phrasal Verbs (general rules)	Past Tenses (selection)

This chart represents the negotiated "syllabus" for the language analysis component of the course, and will be considered and discussed by the whole group. At this point the trainer may ask questions for clarification. e.g. "What is it about *articles* that you find difficult?" The trainer then collects both the overall priority list and the original individual lists of three areas.

3. Between sessions, the trainer checks references in the appropriate grammar, background books, and grammar practice books and does the following things.

   (i) Prepares detailed workcards on the main priority areas listed in the chart. An example of such a workcard is given on page 00.

GRAMMAR WORKCARD
1 ARTICLES

1. Try *TaG* Unit 1, questions 15–19 and refer to *CGE* paragraphs 492–496 as necessary.
2. Take a selective look at *RGSE* Chapter 6, Sections 2–27, focusing on outstanding difficulties.
3. Make a note of any difficulties that have not been dealt with so far.
4. Now look at some student practice exercises (*W to G* Unit 19 and *EGU* Units 69–77) and make a note of any problems or omissions in these exercises, and in the accompanying explanations.
5. What kinds of teaching problem are presented by this language area? What new strategies/ways forward can you develop for work on the article system with your students? Write an awareness-raising exercise for use with one of your classes.

NOTE DOWN ANYTHING WORTH REPORTING TO THE WHOLE GROUP

Key to abbreviations:

   CGE: *A Communicative Grammar of English*, Leech, G and Svartvik, J, 1976
   DE: *Discover English*, Bolitho, R & Tomlinson, B, 1981
   EGU: *English Grammar in Use*, Murphy, R, 1985
   EV: *The English Verb*, Lewis, M, 1986
   MEV: *Meaning and the English Verb*, Leech, G, 1987
   RGSE: *A Reference Grammar for Students of English*, Close, R A, 1975
   TaG: *Talking about Grammar*, Bowers, R G et al, 1987
   W to G: *Ways to Grammar*, Shepherd, J et al, 1984

(ii)   Gives brief references to cover areas listed by individual trainees but not finally included in the overall priority list.

4. In the next session, the trainer brings in prepared workcards along with copies of the reference and practice books mentioned on the cards, and allows for groups/individuals to work on priority areas. This can take place in course time or in the trainees' own time, but there should be opportunities for trainees to ask questions about anything that still puzzles them.

5. Teaching implications are discussed with reference to coursebook units or forthcoming lessons which may perhaps be observed by the trainer. It is particularly useful to discuss any adaptations to coursebook units which may seem necessary in the light of the work done in stage 4.

This procedure also enables the trainer to build up and modify a bank of self-access materials for use in future grammar workshops.

(iii) In-service "refresher" courses for teachers whose first language is not English

Time is always at a premium on these courses, too. Participants often arrive with a "shopping list" of priorities, and with quite disparate expectations about the language work to be covered on the course. Some will (on the surface anyway) be interested in methods or techniques for the presentation and practice of language items, while others may be aware of shortcomings in their own formal command of English. Others still will have a catalogue of questions about language use to put to the teacher trainer. These are often based on worries about the coursebook, which may be perceived as unreliable in certain respects. In addition to all of this, there are often strong psychological factors at play. Some course members may use their competence in English to achieve a measure of ascendancy within the group while others may be nervous about exposing their inadequacies (or what they see as their inadequacies) in a public forum, and may need reassurance. It may be quite difficult to establish common ground, particularly with a mixed nationality group. Once again, the type of modified pyramid discussion outlined above will help to set the agenda. The question to be asked here is a little different: *Which three language points would you most like to see covered on the course?*

Through the filter of the group discussions, a clear set of priorities gradually emerges.

Once this has been established, the approach begins to differ from that used with native-speaker trainees. Teachers whose first language is not English can themselves be classed as advanced learners, and the way into a problem area can usefully be through an exercise for learners, either one focusing on their level (drawn from any of the advanced grammar practice books), or one drawn from a teacher's resource book such as *Grammar in Action* (Rinvolucri, M and Frank C). In either case, a focus on the nature of the exercise can lead usefully to a discussion of points of language use. An inadequate practice exercise may be every bit as useful as a starting point as one which is more reliable, as a discussion of the faults in an exercise will certainly raise all the underlying problems. What follows is an example of an exercise from a grammar practice book *English Grammar in Use*, (Murphy, R), which course members may try out and (with the help of the prompt questions) comment on:

82   *Rod Bolitho*

UNIT 47   Exercises

47.1 *Yesterday you met a friend of yours, Charlie. Charlie told you a lot of things. Here are some of the things he said to you:*

1 I'm thinking of going to live in Canada.

2 My father is in hospital.

3 Nora and Jim are getting married next month.

4 I haven't seen Bill for a while.

5 I've been playing tennis a lot recently.

6 Margaret has had a baby.

7 I don't know what Fred is doing.

8 I hardly ever go out these days.

9 I work 14 hours a day.

10 I'll tell Jim I saw you.

11 You can come and stay with me if you are ever in London.

12 Tom had an accident last week but he wasn't injured.

13 I saw Jack at a party a few months ago and he seemed fine.

Later that day you tell another friend what Charlie said. Use reported speech.

1 Charlie said that he was thinking of going to live in Canada.
2 Charlie said that ....
3 ....
4 ....
5 ....
6 ....
7 ....
8 ....
9 ....
10 ....
11 ....
12 ....
13 ....

47.2 *In this exercise someone says something to you which is the opposite of what they said before. You have to answer* **I thought you said ...**
Example: 'That restaurant is expensive.' 'I thought you said it wasn't expensive.'

1 'Ann is coming to the party.' 'I thought you said she ....'
2 'Bill passed his examination.' 'I thought you said ....'
3 'Ann likes Bill.' 'I thought ....'
4 'I've got many friends.' 'I thought you said you ....'
5 'Jack and Jill are going to get married.' ' ....'
6 'Tom works very hard.' ' ....'
7 'I want to be rich and famous.' ' ....'
8 'I'll be here next week.' ' ....'
9 'I can afford a holiday this year.' ' ....'

1 (in first session)
   Try these two exercises. What do they tell you about the way speech is reported? What do they fail to tell you?

2 (between sessions)
   How is speech reported (a) in everyday conversation? (b) in formal spoken reports? (try listening to "Yesterday in Parliament" on BBC

Radio 4) (c) in newspaper reports? Collect some data and bring it to the next session.

3 (in second session)
What are the important aspects of reported speech for communicative purposes? How far do the following exercises from Murphy deal with the problems you have identified?

UNIT 48 Exercises

48.1 *In this exercise you have to write what you would say in these situations.*
Example: Ann says 'I'm tired'. Five minutes later she says 'Let's play tennis'. What do you say? *You said you were tired*

1 Your friend says 'I'm hungry' so you go to a restaurant. When you get there he says 'I don't want to eat'. What do you say? You said ....
2 Tom tells you 'Ann has gone away'. Later that day you meet her. What do you say? Tom told ....
3 George said 'I don't smoke'. A few days later you see him smoking a cigarette. What do you say to him? You said ....
4 You arranged to meet Jack. He said 'I won't be late'. At last he arrives – 20 minutes late. What do you say? You ....
5 Sue said 'I can't come to the party tonight'. That night you see her at the party. What do you say to her? ....
6 Ann says 'I'm working tomorrow evening'. Later that day she says 'Let's go out tomorrow evening'. What do you say? ....

48.2 *Now you have to complete these sentences with* **said, told** *or* **talked.**
Example: Tom .....*said*.... that he didn't like Brian.

1 Jack .... me that he was enjoying his new job.
2 Tom .... it was a nice restaurant but I didn't like it much.
3 The doctor .... that I would have to rest for at least a week.
4 Mrs Taylor .... us she wouldn't be able to come to the next meeting.
5 Ann .... Tom that she was going away.
6 George couldn't help me. He .... to ask Jack.
7 At the meeting the chairman .... about the problems facing the company.
8 Jill .... us all about her holiday in Australia.

48.3 *Now you have to read a sentence and write a new sentence with the same meaning.*
Examples: 'Listen carefully', he said to us. He told *us to listen carefully.*
'Don't wait for me if I'm late', Ann said.
Ann said *not to wait for her if she was late.*

1 'Eat more fruit and vegetables', the doctor said.
The doctor said ....
2 'Read the instructions before you switch on the machine', he said to me.
He told ....
3 'Shut the door but don't lock it', she said to us.
She told ....
4 'Can you speak more slowly? I can't understand', he said to me.
He asked .... because ....
5 'Don't come before 6 o'clock', I said to him.
I told ....

---

4 What else is there for you to teach about reported speech? How would you go about it? (small group discussion, reporting back)

Most teachers whose first language is not English share a common curiosity about the English language, and so it is always a legitimate topic for discussion. They particularly enjoy, and profit from, the innovative, semantically-based approach of *Talking About Grammar* but also appreciate the ideas in supplementary materials such as *Grammar in Action.*

As teachers, we should remain lifelong students of the language we teach. One function of awareness activities is to develop and maintain a healthy spirit of enquiry which, in turn, will lead to new discoveries about language and new ways of looking at old problems. At the same time, such activities should sharpen a teacher's critical faculties, enabling her/him to conduct thorough explorations of language points for teaching purposes, and to be more aware of flaws in coursebooks and difficulties which learners may encounter. The confidence a teacher gains from acquiring these abilities is a vital element in meeting the demands of teaching language for communication.

References

*Bolitho, R and Tomlinson, B 1981 *Discover English*. Heinemann, London

*Bowers, R G et al 1987 *Talking about Grammar*. Longman, London

Close, R A 1975 *A Reference Grammar for Students of English*. Longman, London

Eastwood, J and Mackin, R 1982 *A Basic English Grammar*. OUP, Oxford

Leech, G 1987 *Meaning and the English Verb*. Longman, London

Leech, G and Svartvik J 1976 *A Communicative Grammar of English*. Longman, London

Lewis, M 1986 *The English Verb*. Language Teaching Publications, Hove

Murphy, R 1985 *English Grammar in Use*. CUP, Cambridge

Rinvolucri, M and Frank C 1983 *Grammar in Action*. Pergamon, Oxford

Shepherd, J et al 1984 *Ways to Grammar*. Macmillan, Basingstoke

(*these titles contain language awareness activities)

9

Norman Whitney reflects on developments in the teaching of reading over twenty-five years, on how it has been dealt with in training courses, and teases out the wider implications in relation to fundamental questions of teacher education.

He points out that some of the most significant influences (e.g. the question of literacy, design and typography) which have encouraged thinking of reading as a process and skill have come from outside ELT, and he is critical of "the tendency of ELT to isolate itself from the world of education in general", suggesting that unacknowledged debts are ones which have not been honoured in terms of either understanding or action.

The article also points to the danger of teacher training in EFL being merely an internally self-referring process in which trainers and trainees take part in a closed dialogue that simply "refers" to the classroom. The frequent lack of opportunity for trainees to give feedback to institutions about how well their training equipped them for teaching highlights the danger.

The present interest in teacher education as a broad concept and teacher development give reason to hope that wider perspectives are gradually being taken by many involved in the preparation of EFL teachers.

Of Shoeboxes and Broom Cupboards:

Reading, twenty-five years on

NORMAN WHITNEY

The 1960s

Powerful traditions are rejected

Twenty-five years ago scant attention was given in ELT to the idea that reading is a skill at all. The long-established powerful influences exerted by grammar translation procedures were on the whole inimical to anything but the idea that reading involved much more than careful word-by-word, highly concentrated forms of comprehension work. For the minority of students who managed to progress to advanced classes, the concept of reading was broadened a little, but only to the extent that extensive reading was for the clever student, and meant reading "proper" literature. The power of this tradition was, and still is, enormous. Today, it still controls the perception of modern language learning and teaching in some universities, and not just in the UK.

In the second part of the 1960s, the pressures exerted by behaviourist theories of learning resulted in the use of texts in which the grammar, vocabulary and discourse features were very carefully controlled. Experts and teachers advocated the supremacy of habit formation through oral work (drilling), teacher performance and objective testing. This second tradition was largely initiated in America, and it reached large numbers of people in a very short time. One result was that, in some circles, the reading of literature fell rapidly out of favour. This fall from grace in effect deprived at least some students of practically their only source of extensive, authentic reading matter.

The provision of reading material was characterised by texts which were either wholly artificial, or which, if real, were usually fragments on the one hand, or whole literary works on the other. Texts were visually bare, and often unsatisfactorily decontextualised. The language of such texts was more often used for extra work on grammar and vocabulary – even on pronunciation – than for reading, or even reading comprehension, as such. And a tendency for exercises to draw freely on a wide range of exercise types was quite confusing. The mixture of yes/no questions, information questions, blank-filling tasks, spot the spelling mistake activities, was not helpful. All of this encouraged students, quite reasonably, to approach reading comprehension as a form of extended general language practice.

A crucial feature of this type of work was that both teachers and students found themselves using the results of this kind of comprehension work to make very important but unsound judgements that did not concern reading at all. So students who got "ten out of ten" or "three out of ten" were thought to be good or bad not only in respect of reading comprehension, but also in respect of English *in toto*.

Despite the reservations that some teachers had about this tendency to use the marks for traditional reading comprehension exercises as an indicator of general proficiency in English, the tendency received tremendous support from researchers, especially in the States. This was certainly the case with the mass of research data about the reliability and validity of multiple choice as a way of testing reading comprehension. The influence of the research has had an enormous influence together with a washback effect, firstly on teacher training, secondly on teaching and thirdly on materials, including those used for examinations such as First Certificate and Proficiency. This washback effect nourished the idea that reading comprehension really did consist of "not very interesting texts followed by even less interesting questions". Clearly then, the "decontextualised text followed by multiple choice questions" approach to reading comprehension held its ground for quite a long time. That was partly because it received all the kudos that so-called objective research sometimes provides.

The 1970s

A kind of progress

A lot of real progress in our understanding of reading and its teaching was made in the 1970s. As a result ELT teachers now readily perceive of reading as a macro-skill in itself, comprised of a number of micro-skills that relate to each other. This perception may or may not reflect reality (who knows?), but it has certainly proved procedurally useful and of help to students.

The notional/functional movement of the 1970s in particular freed reading comprehension activities from some of the restrictive practices that had held them in the grip of "translateability" and tight structural and lexical control. The result was a greater degree of interest in texts that were "authentic" and which demonstrated the sorts of notions and functions (usually the latter) that students were believed to need. Exercises began to reflect more accurately the reading processes and the real life activities that would normally accompany such texts.

Methods of presentation, practice, and assessment moved away from reading aloud and teacher-directed questioning towards the package of techniques usually referred to as pre-reading, while-reading and post-reading activities (see, for example, Barr, Clegg and Wallace 1981). These included discussions, questions, exercises, tasks – all of which were plausibly generated by texts, and which together attempted to reflect the actual use of texts in life. The power of "doing well" in reading comprehension as an indicator of overall language proficiency slipped. Getting the right answer in reading comprehension exercises was no longer the same as learning English well. Quite the reverse: the idea was that doing well in reading comprehension meant precisely that – becoming a good reader.

Those working within the British and European tradition of ELT developed their feelings about reading on the basis of interest in the reading process itself, of convictions about the importance of student need, of experience of actual classes and of common sense rather than on empirical research data alone. Except for the tremendous influence of a small number of books about reading (which did of course include important research work), the progress made in the 1970s depended very much for its development and energy on a spirit of adventure, on an inclination to take risks, and on the insights and encouragement provided by the work of, *inter alia*, the following. On reading: Goodman 1968, Smith 1971, Kohl 1973, Lunzer and Gardener 1979; on readability, design and typography: Gilliland 1972, McLean 1980; on discourse and stylistics: Halliday and Hassan 1976, Widdowson 1974, 1975; on applications to language learning and teaching: The Council of Europe 1973, Wilkins 1976, Widdowson 1978; on self-assessment: Oskarsson 1978; and numbers of teachers, trainers, authors and publishers whose contributions and motives were, to say the least, varied.

Not all of these influences were of the theoretical or applied linguistic kind. Some were much more of the educational kind, and others were the product of conviction and inspiration, exercised without the benefit of empirical evidence. Some of these influences, especially those dealing with design and typography, were not at all directly concerned with ELT. Non-ELT influences on our perception and teaching of reading were and in my opinion still are, more important to ELT than many appreciate. The various handbooks of the current decade (see, for example Grellet 1981, Nuttall 1982, Williams 1984) do not always make this point very seriously. Interesting though these recent handbooks are, they tend to follow as much as they lead, and they tend to confirm as much as they reveal. Except for Nuttall's extremely helpful book, they have also tended to draw on ELT sources alone. Inevitably, they may have given at least some EFL teachers the impression that, somehow, ELT "discovered" reading. It didn't.

It is this last point – the tendency for ELT to isolate itself from the world of education in general – that is one signal of the extent to which the progress made in the 1970s in the teaching of reading was not, in fact, as great as we would like to believe.

There was then and there still is today a general sense in which the debt that EFL owes to non-ELT influences for this knowledge of reading is largely unacknowledged, and therefore not fully understood nor yet fully acted on. This is not to suggest that we should be looking back all the time, or that an understanding of the history of reading is a *sine qua non* of its successful teaching. But a consideration of this debt owed by ELT to other areas of interest would have the advantage of demonstrating links between mainstream EFL and those areas such as the teaching of reading in L1 contexts, the teaching of reading to children, the acquisition of reading skills in bilingual, multilingual and multicultural contexts, and, very importantly, the question of literacy.

An appreciation of these links is very important, especially for example for those teachers and teacher trainers in mainstream adult ELT who profess an interest in the teaching of EFL to young children. At the moment, there is a tendency for existing expertise in the teaching of ELT to adults to transform itself, merely on the basis of demand, into expertise in the teaching of EFL to children. Such transformations are based on assumptions which are questionable. One of these is that the progress made in mainstream adult EFL teaching is real enough, powerful enough and adequate enough to justify the "can do" spirit of many of its practitioners. I suggest that from the point of view of reading, the requirements and procedures for adults and children in ELT are likely to be more different than many of us realise. Such differences represent one aspect of ELT that much of the training provision in the UK has so far failed to come to terms with.

A properly researched assessment of our assumptions about progress in the teaching of reading could reveal that any such progress has in fact been more marked in training sessions than in actual classes. New trainee teachers are taken up to the same certain useful points, but not always beyond. It is in fact quite easy to subscribe to (sometimes blind) convictions about authenticity, pre-reading, appropriate tasks and so on in training sessions. But it is worth remembering that the opportunities for new teachers to come back two years later and tell us we got it all wrong are not great, especially if their training had been with multilingual classes, yet their first job with monolingual classes, or vice versa. We all know that in practice, the management of authentic texts, pre-reading, post-reading and so on is actually often very hard to implement, especially for relatively inexperienced teachers, and for the large numbers of elementary and lower intermediate students who are reading in order to improve their grammar and vocabulary!

There are still many classes in which there is the familiar syndrome of "nice text, pity about the questions!". That usually means that the text may be authentic, but the exercises aren't at all, with the result that the text is not, to use Widdowson's useful term (1979, 1984), being "authenticated" in any way. We know too that there are many classes in which students of all levels demand their right to know the meanings of individual words and phrases and in which teachers, despite exhortations from their training, monopolise the asking of the post-text questions. There is no doubt either that even trained teachers still regularly stop the reading process in order to explain grammar points, vocabulary and idioms.

These classroom procedures which, on the face of it, are counter to a lot of the received wisdom passed around on training courses, could be much more common than trainers realise. If this guess about what actually goes on in classes is right, the problem lies not with teachers, and especially not with those teachers who are recently trained or relatively inexperienced. The problem lies with trainers and training.

The implications of a situation in which training, especially initial training, regularly subscribes to sets of attitudes and procedures which, in practice, are more often honoured in the breach than in the observance, are serious. The problem could be that, for trainers, the rewards of saying what they feel to be right and sensible are quite simply more immediately accessible than is the trick of converting what they say into what their trainees can actually do. This is a classic dilemma in training of any sort, and is not peculiar to EFL. It may also be that, at least as far as reading is concerned, training has pitched its expectations too high of what new teachers can do and what some students will tolerate. Either way, unless trainers are in a position to follow up their trainees and to see how the training is actually transferred to classroom practice, yet another asymmetrical relationship between training and practice will develop very rapidly, even after initial training courses. This would lead to a further example in the profession of the difficulty of reconciling theory and practice.

One solution to this sort of problem is to adopt the sort of rigorous internal inspection procedures conducted by large organisations such as International House. One of the strengths of the International House training scheme has been that the organisation produces its own teachers and then lives with them. There is of course a risk that this could create a self-fulfilling prophecy, or that it could create a self-perpetuating, but illusory, image of quality. But in practice, what has actually happened is that the work of its own teachers has at its best provided the International House training network with a form of feedback on the training process itself.

The 1980s

New trends

The communicative orthodoxy of the 1970s has given way to a number of newer preferences and trends. These are concerned with a number of different issues, some of which, as might be expected, are likely to prove less influential in the development of reading than others.

1. Eclecticism

These days, the "L" in EFL is eclectic. It is not exclusively structural, and it is certainly not exclusively functional. It is, somehow, both of these, though – as if clinging to the remnants of received wisdom in the previous decade – it is also still desirably "communicative". It is, despite what teachers might say and wish, in practice largely coursebook governed. The preference at the moment is clearly for coursebooks that are compendium-esque. The popular coursebooks of today are those that seem to be able to do a bit of everything: structures, functions, grammar, vocabulary, pronunciation, speaking, listening, reading, writing, study skills. And precisely because they do have a bit of everything, they provide a convenient basis for syllabuses. Indeed, in some schools, they are the syllabus itself. This is true even on short courses, where an individual student's progress and a teacher's work may still be defined in terms of the completion of rather long units from a long book.

The reading component of the all-purpose coursebook is based on texts which are long enough to demonstrate both structures and functions, but short enough to be dealt with by the teacher in single lessons or, in order to provide variety and pace, in only parts of single lessons. At the same time, the texts are designed in a manner that allows them to pass for authentic since, in many circles, that requirement is still highly favoured. The impression that texts of this type have reintroduced the elements of textual control and elements of the traditional, word-by-word reading comprehension of two decades ago, is confirmed by the exercises, by no means all or even most of which are reading skills related. In one of the most popular mainstream courses students are regularly advised to "read this with a dictionary". "This" may well be a story, an amusing anecdote, or life-and-institutions type information. But the text is not only there to be read, if at all, as part of a programme of skills development of reading fluency, but often as a test of the comprehension of individual words, or as the springboard for yet more practice in structure and grammar. In order to perform these roles, individual texts carry inauthentically abundant examples of the grammatical point at issue, (see Swan and Walter, 1984).

The problem is that the sum total of texts in such a coursebook may be necessary reading for the student following just that course, but it is by no means sufficient – as I am sure the authors I have referred to would agree – for the development of the reading skill outside it. But whereas in earlier days it was recognised that any coursebook had its selective linguistic bias, which needed to be supplemented by "readers" and reading materials, there is today a sense in which, because it seems to do a bit of everything, the modern all-purpose coursebook appears to have all but eliminated that need. The notion of eclecticism has got mixed up with the related but different notion of comprehensiveness, with the result that such materials may well be increasing teachers' dependence on coursebooks for their day-to-day supply of reading matter for their students.

Curiously, then, the popularity of the eclectic coursebook may prove to have taken the teaching of reading back somewhat. Indeed, from the point of view of reading, it could be that the full-blown communicative courses and materials of a decade ago were rather more useful to students than are the "do-it-all" courses of today because, in their sometimes cavalier treatment of grammar and vocabulary, some communicative materials of the 1970s found it easier to provide reading texts which were relatively unconstrained syntactically and lexically, and which were therefore potentially worth "reading". The general and valid assumption of a decade ago that coursebooks were indeed partial usually provoked teachers into looking out for supplementary materials, especially for reading, that covered the sort of ground that, by general agreement, the coursebook did not.

2. Teacher development and affective/humanistic approaches

Turning to the current interest in teacher development and the interest in affective and humanistic approaches, it may be rather shocking – and unfair – to suggest that these two most important interests may prove inimical to the further development of reading. These suggestions are only impressions, and by no means represent any criticism of either interest: they are merely reflections on their possible usefulness or otherwise to reading.

Teacher development, though ostensibly dedicated to the service of learners, not unnaturally deals with teachers themselves. Discussions in TD groups about straightforward, practical classroom procedures for reading may not be wholly appropriate or looked for. Teacher development discussions are sometimes constrained by their need to be disassociated from "training" and linked much more to "development", though the distinction between the two is inevitably not always clear. This constraint is a product, presumably, of teachers in such groups feeling themselves to be already rather more highly trained than they are – to use a somewhat less happy collocation – highly developed.

Again, similarly, affective and humanistic approaches have as their legitimate concern a whole range of issues of which the teaching of reading may not be one, or at least a prominent one. At the 1987 IATEFL/TESOL Summer Institute in Barcelona, for example, there were teachers who had degrees and diplomas in suggestopaedia and other humanistic approaches. Yet, faced with the prospect of employment in China, these qualified teachers had suddenly to come to terms with the fact that at no time in their particular programmes had they discussed the management of reading in classes. I doubt that this was representative of such training elsewhere, but it was nonetheless the case for participants in my course in Barcelona.

The real problem between teacher development/humanistic interests and the teaching of reading is that there is no necessary relationship between the two. As a teacher, I could become highly developed, as well as highly trained, and I could, to the approval of my peers, become humanistically sound. But in neither case would this necessarily give any indication of an interest or proficiency in managing reading. None of this would matter if it weren't for the fact that, at the moment there is tremendous pressure on teachers to become either or both developed and humanistic. Just as teachers two decades ago felt that they had to spend a lot of time studying linguistics, so many now feel a need to explore themselves.

Such pressures may be very useful, if only because they signal real movements and developments, and because they make explicit some of the evolving initiation and continuing membership rites that any professional group sets up for itself. Such rites confer prestige, approval and membership on some, and they confer opprobrium, disapproval and exclusion on others. To that extent, the EFL profession is indeed much like any other, despite its protestations about being liberal, progressive, and non-judgemental. But it is not at all clear that from the limited point of view of reading, such pressures are actually very helpful to students. Sadly, if the successful teaching of reading is not the sort of activity that can yield visible evidence of developed, humanistic attitudes and practices, then teachers who are interested in the teaching of reading, and indeed teachers who do it very well, may look in vain to their developed, humanistic colleagues for peer group recognition and support.

3. L1/L2 relationships

There is evidence today of a greater sensitivity on the part of native speaker teachers of English towards the first language of their students. Some teacher-training institutions in the UK, with access only to multilingual classes, have been a little slow in coming to terms with the crucial fact that most classes in the world are in fact monolingual. Indeed, many teachers whose first language is English have been able to disguise their lack of proficiency in any foreign language at all, let alone the language of any particular group of students they are working with. Many such teachers and teacher trainers have elevated "the direct method" into high art. But attitudes are changing, and along with changing attitudes, there are changing priorities about practical procedures for managing monolingual classes. It is no longer fashionable to ignore translation.

For the teaching of reading, this resurgence of interest in the students' first language could be good, because it means that a sensitively organised reading programme can legitimately take into account specific features of linguistic ease, interest and difficulty.

4. Cross-cultural awareness

A reading programme that takes into account students' first language and their proficiency in it can address more general questions about the cultural and educational relevance of the reading material made available to them. Reading material that is targeted at the existing knowledge, assumptions and indeed prejudices of its readers seems on the face of it much more likely to succeed than randomly chosen texts that are given to students merely because such texts happen to appear in Unit X of yet another global course or reading comprehension course Y. It is certainly the case that the careful study of the cross-cultural implications has, until recently, been much more taken on board by those working in ESL.

5. Learner training and development

The greatest opportunities for development in the provision of reading material and tasks probably lie with the current growth of interest in learner training and development. This area of interest is not in fact all that new. Aspects of learner training dealing with self-assessment for example, have been in evidence for quite some time (e.g. Oskarsson op. cit. 1978, Dickinson and Carver 1980, Davies and Whitney, 1984). But more recently a mass of research into the good learner and apparently good language learning strategies have recently become more accessible, as, for example, in the work of Wenden (1986), and in the work by Dickinson on self-directed learning (1987).

The models provided by recent research, and a conviction that the focus in EFL should shift from the teacher to the learner now means that more and more teachers are simply going to their students and finding out what, how, and why they read. On the basis of their findings, teachers can provide their students with a reading programme that makes sense and that is far more satisfactory than the spare diet provided by even the best coursebooks and conventional supplementary materials. In practice, the usefulness of such introspection lies not only in the truth or otherwise of what students tell us, but in the act of trying to discover that truth, and in the process of negotiation and consultation between teachers and students that such discussions generate.

A warning, however. A learner-centred approach to reading will often mean that the texts and activities that students really find valuable and interesting turn out to be more varied and unpredictable than most teachers expect. Given a wide range of choice, students just do not go for the sorts of reading matter that we imagine they can cope with, or even that we think they should cope with. Depending on how you set things up, students choose to read both above and below their presumed language level, and they often engross themselves in topics (e.g. the royal family) which a lot of teachers, especially in mainstream adult EFL teaching in the UK, just can't or don't want to deal with. "From Grantham to Greatness: the story of the Honourable Mrs Margaret Thatcher" may not be every teacher's idea of stimulating reading; but students might love it!

6. *Self-access systems*

Self-access has already become something of a slogan, and some of what passes as self-access work is probably not really that at all: it can just be a new way of referring to self-study or even be "EFL-ese" for what used to be called library space. Still, many teachers are very much in favour of the idea of self-access, and for reading, this is good news.

At the risk of suggesting the obvious, I would recommend to those teachers who have not yet tried it, running a self-access or at least a "self-determined" class library. This is a useful way of watching the reading preferences of your students shift and develop, and it is an interesting exercise in one sort of learner training and development. Class libraries can be stocked with any number of items, including of course all the non-authentic, semi-authentic books that are variously described as graded readers, structural readers and so on, (see Hill and Thomas 1988).

Of course, as everyone knows, many of the titles discussed by Hill and Thomas have been around for a long time, and such titles anyway represent only a fraction of the material that a class library can include. Even so, it may be that relatively few teachers have exploited the graded reader resource as fully as possible. This is particularly the case in those schools and colleges where such material, has been consigned to a formal, centralised borrowing system, (or even to a well-organised, but school-based self-access centre) rather than set up as an informal localised, classroom-based facility. These start as it were from nothing and then, by dint of choice and selection, grow into something – and, at the end of the course or term, disappear into nothing again, only to be reborn, phoenix-like, with another class, on another occasion.

Centralised borrowing systems are often less efficient than class-room-based borrowing systems. This is because conventional libraries find it very difficult to handle individual little books, and because many students are intimidated by libraries, librarians, and row upon row of books which they have been told are "good for them". Neither does a centralised borrowing system provide students with an immediate opportunity to select what goes into the pool of reading materials, or to share their reading experiences with the rest of the class, or with the teacher. Without the encouragement and feedback that fellow students and teachers can provide, many students seem to find that searching a library for something manageable to read, and then reading it, is actually more trouble than it's worth.

For teachers to build in the sort of classroom behaviour that accompanies the running of a class library, they may have to reorganise their lesson plans rather drastically, and they may have to modify their ideas about definitions of good practice in their work. This is because even a relatively small and apparently simple innovation in the classroom requires some adjustment of everything else – as anyone who has tried to implement self-study and self-access facilities knows. (For suggestions about how to implement class libraries, see the excellent book by Hedge 1985.)

7. The integration of language, content and project work

Teachers who choose to run self-generating class libraries in their full-blown form may also have to sacrifice some of the time that is spent with coursebooks, and work with their directors of studies on new models of syllabus design, especially for short courses. The inclusion in syllabuses of, for example, a request that each student might read a number of texts of whatever length and type (and provide a written or oral summary of any one title) would surely help to break the grip on such syllabuses of conventional coursebooks.

Such requirements could easily be built into the sort of course that actively attempts to link language with content. Syllabuses of that sort are ideally suited to short courses. They lend a touch of choice and variety to the work of both students and teachers and lead to the idea that syllabuses can be expressed in terms of, say, the completion of interesting performance objectives, real life tasks, class projects and so on. Examples of this latter type of syllabus are described by Carter and Thomas (1986) and the content-related courses on "Film Studies" and "the Press and Media" at International House London.

The rationale and implications for content-led work in ELT repay all the time and effort that they involve, especially for the development of reading skills. The integration of language and content does not have to take the rather hard-headed, educationally restricted shape that it does in some versions of ESP, as work in adult ESL and in the language across the curriculum movement in schools has shown. There are already handbooks and teachers' guides for mainstream ELT teachers on the subject of language and content (e.g. Mohan 1986), and there has been some research work on its implications for the teaching of reading (Carrell 1987). All of these tend to confirm the reasoning behind some major recent coursebooks (for children) in which the integration of language and content has been attempted not only in a global context (Abbs and Freebairn 1986) but also in the context of a cross-curricular approach to students in one country (Whitney and Dandini 1988).

Conclusion

A qualified request for empirical research

Now is the time perhaps for the teaching of reading in EFL to take advantage of the current fashion for empirical research into second language acquisition (SLA), even though, for the empirical investigation of reading, the sheer inaccessibility of data must be a source of endless frustration to researchers. Interestingly, Ellis' very helpful 1985 "state of the art" summary of SLA does not identify reading as such as a separate area of inquiry at all: it is not separated in the way that, for example, classroom language, first language transfer, and memorisation are. On the face of it, this apparent lack of consideration given to reading in such work suggests how incredibly limited the notion of input in such research might be.

And even where there have been experiments about reading in EFL/ESL, the conclusions are not always particularly revealing. For example, the very interesting research done by Carrell on the role of background knowledge, schemata and rhetorical organisation (1983, 1984) tends to confirm principles that have been familiar to teachers for generations – a point that she herself more or less acknowledges in a recent paper (op. cit. 1987).

The problem however is that the assumptions and procedures, and perhaps therefore the conclusions, of such research are more open to question than is often admitted. For example, Carrell writes that "In empirical tests of these two different types of schemata (content and form), it is fairly easy to separate out and to test for the effects of one type, while holding the effects of the other type constant." (1987 p 461). This claim is not as unprejudiced as it looks. Certainly, Carrell makes her experiments sound easy and simple to set up. Her experimental designs are neat and manageable. They are so manageable in fact that her concepts of text, meaning, rhetoric culture are vulnerable to the charge that they are a trifle unsophisticated and selective. Her decision, though qualified and hedged, to choose religion as the basis for defining cultural background ("Catholic" and "Muslim", 1987), is rather alarming and potentially a dangerous one: is there, then, a Protestant reading culture? An atheist one? Jewish?) And her tendency to exclude from her experiments much appreciation of the role in reading of typography, design and layout is also problematic, since it seems to eliminate from consideration a crucial factor in the reading process.

So if empirical research on reading and SLA is to be carried out, and if it is to prove as helpful as the mass of empirical and non-empirical research on reading that has gone before, it must take into account many variables. It may also have to bear in mind that its findings can easily be abused. Peter Skehan, (in a lecture given at IH called "Second Language acquisition: where are we up to?" March, 1987) has claimed that the value of research lies in its capacity to prevent and check "extremes" of one sort or another. I am not sure. My own impression is that research and researchers have created as many extremes as they have prevented, and that they have given some extremes a patina of respectability and a not always justified glow of academic integrity. Research is research: but it is also a powerful weapon in the politics of education and advancement.

Interestingly, in his plenary TESOL address of 1985, Stephen Krashen chose reading and books as his main theme. But eschewing many of the precepts of empirical research, and avoiding the trap of too many experiments, findings, conclusions, statistics, data and so on, he simply argued that books and reading are "a good thing". He said that large amounts of varied reading materials should be made available to large numbers of students at whatever cost, and if necessary, in preference to, for example, the expense of providing those students with computers.

That message was refreshingly unacademic and low tech. It was an interesting example of someone with great influence seizing the opportunity to say something sensible clearly and with great conviction. After all, as any teacher knows, you can get an awful lot of books and other reading matter for students into a shoebox, and you can get an awful lot of shoeboxes into even the smallest broom cupboard.

References

This list includes only publications referred to in the chapter. It is not intended to be an exhaustive bibliography about reading.

Abbs, B. and Freebairn, I. (1986) *Discoveries*. London: Longman.

Barr, P., Clegg, J. and Wallace, C. (1981) *Advanced Reading Skills in English*. London: Longman.

Carrell, P. (1983) 'Background knowledge in second language comprehension.' *Language Learning and Communication*, Vol 2, No 1.

Carrell, P. (1983) 'Some issues in studying the role of schemata, or background knowledge, in second language comprehension.' *Reading in a Foreign Language*, Vol 1, No 2.

Carrell, P. (1983) 'Three components of background knowledge in reading comprehension.' *Language Learning*, Vol 33, No 2.

Carrell, P. (1983) (with Eisterhold) 'Schema theory and ESL reading pedagogy.' *TESOL Quarterly*, Vol 17, No 4.

Carrell, P. (1984) 'Evidence of a formal scheme in second language comprehension.' *Language Learning*, Vol 34, No 2.

Carrell, P. (1984) 'The effects of rhetorical organization on ESL readers.' *TESOL Quarterly*, Vol 18, No 3.

Carrell, P. (1987) 'Content and Formal Schemata in ESL Reading.' *TESOL Quarterly*, Vol 21, No 3.

Carter, G. and Thomas, H. (1986) ' 'Dear Brown Eyes . . .': experiential learning in a project oriented approach.' *English Language Teaching Journal*, Vol 40, No 3. Oxford: Oxford University Press and The British Council.

Davies, E. and Whitney, N. (1984) *Study Skills for Reading*. London: Heinemann Educational Books.

Dickinson, L. and Carver, D. (1980) 'Learning to Learn: steps towards self direction in foreign languages in schools.' *English Language Teaching Journal*: Vol 35 No 1.

Dickinson, L. (1987) *Self Instruction in Language Learning*. Cambridge: Cambridge University Press.

Ellis, R. (1985) *Understanding Second Language Acquisition*. Oxford: Oxford University Press.

Gilliland, J. (1972) *Readability.* London: University of London Press for the United Kingdom Reading Association.

Goodman, K. S. (editor) (1968) *The Psycholinguistic Nature of the Reading Process.* Detroit: Wayne State University Press.

Grellet, F. (1981) *Developing Reading Skills.* Cambridge: Cambridge University Press.

Halliday, M. A. K. and Hassan, R. (1976) *Cohesion in English.* London: Longman.

Hedge, T. (1985) *Using Readers in Language Teaching.* London: Macmillan.

Hill, D. R. and Thomas, H. Reid (1988) Survey Review: 'Graded Readers.' *English Language Teaching Journal.* Part 1, Vol 42, No 1, Part 2, Vol 42, No 2. Oxford: Oxford University Press and The British Council.

Kohl, H. (1973) *Reading, How To.* New York: Dutton.

Lunzer, E. and Gardner, K. (1979) *The Effective Use of Reading.* London: Heinemann Educational Books for the Schools Council.

McLean, R. (1980) *The Thames and Hudson Manual of Typography.* London: Thames and Hudson.

Mohan, Bernard (1986) *Language and Content.* New York: Addison Wesley.

Nuttall, C. (1982) *Teaching Reading Skills in a Foreign Language.* London: Heinemann Educational Books.

Oskarsson, M. (1978) *Approaches to self-assessment in foreign language learning.* Strasbourg: Council for Cultural Cooperation, Council of Europe.

Smith, F. (1971) *Understanding Reading.* New York: Holt, Rinehart and Winston.

Swan, M. and Walter, C. (1984) Practice Book 1: *The Cambridge English Course.* Cambridge: Cambridge University Press.

The Council of Europe (1973) *Systems Development in Adult Language Learning.* Strasbourg: Council for Cultural Cooperation, Council of Europe.

Wenden, A. (1986) 'Helping language learners think about learning.' *English Language Teaching Journal* Vol 40, No 1. Oxford: Oxford University Press and The British Council.

Whitney, N. and Dandini, M. G. (1988) *Adventures in English: a communicative, interdisciplinary course for the Italian scuola media.* Oxford/Firenze: Oxford University Press/La Nuova Italia.

Widdowson, H. G. (1974) 'Stylistics' in Corder and Allen (eds) *The Edinburgh Course in Applied Linguistics*, Vol 3. Oxford: Oxford University Press.

Widdowson, H. G. (1975) *Stylistics and the Teaching of Literature.* London: Longman.

Widdowson, H. G. (1978) *Teaching Language as Communication.* Oxford: Oxford University Press.

Widdowson, H. G. (1979) *Explorations in Applied Linguistics.* Oxford: Oxford University Press.

Widdowson, H. G. (1984) *Explorations in Applied Linguistics 2.* Oxford: Oxford University Press.

Wilkins, D. (1976) *Notional Syllabuses.* Oxford: Oxford University Press.

Williams, E. (1984) *Reading in the Language Classroom.* London: Macmillan.

10 Establishing clear criteria for the selection of teacher educators is one of the most difficult and important factors in running successful and effective programmes for the preparation of teachers.

In certain circumstances the difficulty lies in educators and trainers having been self-selected – by dint of seeing a need, being willing, and feeling capable of undertaking the task. The urge to share ideas and experience in response to a need is by no means necessarily a bad base from which to start, but nonetheless in practice it can lead to quite unsuitable people placing themselves in positions of educational influence.

The stages of preparation of educators and trainers are in some senses part of the selection process, in that a novice may be judged to need more extended preparation or, if proving to be inadequate to the demands of the task, may even have to be withdrawn. Such judgements are particularly difficult to make because they frequently involve colleagues (i.e. teacher-training tutors to whom the notice has been "attached") making professional judgements on each other. (Peter Maingay's article on "Observation for Training Development and Assessment" is relevant to this question.)

Richard Rossner offers an overview of different types of EFL teacher education as a background to the criteria that must be taken into account when selecting new staff for courses.

Selecting Teacher Educators

– establishing criteria

RICHARD ROSSNER

This article considers the selection of staff for teacher education in English as a foreign language, and perhaps by extension for other kinds of foreign language-teacher education. Its purpose is to recommend a thorough and well-considered approach to selection, preparation and induction of teacher educators since their role and responsibility in the development of language teaching and learning is so crucial. I hasten to add that what I have to say is not inspired by any grave disquiet about what is going on in EFL teacher education. Rather, it reflects the fact that more and more formal EFL teacher education is taking place as the demand for English increases world-wide and as professional awareness develops.

Types of EFL teacher education

The term "teacher education" is used to include skill – or technique-focused programmes with mainly practical orientation (teacher training), programmes that aim to develop the confidence, awareness, self-reliance and self-esteem of practising teachers (teacher development), and programmes that combine various focuses and might imply a one-year full time commitment (e.g. certain MA or Diploma programmes). The terminological problems are symptomatic of what is, world-wide, a complex pattern of provision.

Initial teacher education

Programmes that aim to enable people who are not teachers, or are not EFL teachers, to teach English as a foreign language at school level or in further education, fall into four categories:

 i) components or modules in postgraduate (in Britain, for example, PGCE) programmes or in undergraduates degrees (e.g. B.Ed) at universities.
 ii) similar components of long term courses at teacher-training colleges, known in some countries as "normal" schools.
 iii) short courses leading to "recognised" qualifications guaranteed by examining boards or other bodies (in Britain, the Royal Society of Arts Preparatory Certificate is an example).
 iv) short (and not so short) courses offered by specific institutions to allcomers, or perhaps only to teachers who are to work at the institution in question. Normally such courses lead only to an institutional certificate. Good examples of such courses are to be found at certain Latin American binational Cultura institutes.

It has to be admitted, however, that a very large number of EFL teachers, whether native speakers of English or not, begin teaching English with no prior training at all, and in many countries it is still common for EFL and other language teachers to begin service with no more competence to do so than that implied by a degree in English literature, a Cambridge Certificate of Proficiency in English, or, in the case of native speakers, their mother tongue. This does not necessarily mean that they will work ineffectively or incompetently – at least, as someone who started EFL teaching at age 17 I hope not! But it does make the next category of teacher education that much more crucial.

Post experience and in-service teacher education

By far the most common type of in-service teacher education is institution-based or sponsored by an education board or authority. It usually takes the form of staff meetings, workshops and seminars, and (apart from purely administrative issues) the aims are usually related to the preoccupations of educational planners, materials writers and senior staff in the institutions or authorities . However, increasingly teachers' own concerns and requirements are being taken into account. Teachers are consulted about these programmes and perhaps given responsibility in the design and running of them. Moreover, teachers themselves are taking the initiative and organising their own in-service sessions (see, for example, recent issues of the IATEFL special interest group publication *Teacher Development*). In addition, regional, national and international teachers associations are flourishing and can make a valuable (if infrequent and sporadic) contribution to in-service teacher education.

This type of provision is crucially important, but its true impact cannot be measured and is likely to vary dramatically from system to system and from institution to institution. Differing levels of support mean that some teachers are deterred from fully committing themselves because of lack of "space" in their working week, or in the case of some longer-term government sponsored programmes, the lack of career incentive. It is not realistic, for example, to expect teachers to give up evenings or whole weekend days to pursue a national or regional refresher or retraining programme if it is not going to make any difference to their salaries or career prospects in the longer term.

Other post-experience courses fall into the following main categories:

i) postgraduate courses (e.g. Diplomas, MAs and research degrees) which aim to increase participants' knowledge and understanding of "informing disciplines" such as applied linguistics and psychology while developing the breadth and depth of their language teaching practice. Usually these do not include teaching practice.

ii) part-time and intensive courses leading, for example, to Royal Society of Arts diplomas. Such courses do include teaching practice.

iii) institution or system-based programmes leading to internal certification or "upgrading".

Complicating factors

This sketchplan of EFL teacher education is further complicated by the following factors:

i)   different types of participant group: some are homogeneous (e.g. all from the same level in the same national educational system), and some heterogeneous (as on "open enrolment" courses in Britain). In post-experience courses, this may mean that little or none of the previous experience gained by different participants is equivalent in type or duration, and that the teaching contexts participants are being prepared to cope with differ radically.

ii) differing lengths of course and modes of instruction: there is a world of difference not just between longer (e.g. 200 hour) courses and shorter (e.g. 40 hour) ones, but also between full-time and part-time courses, where, in the case of initial training, the time available between sessions may allow greater opportunities for assimilation and adjustment. Moreover, if as in many universities and teacher-training colleges the main contact with educators is through lectures and academic papers, the impact may be different from courses in which lectures are mixed with workshops, demonstrations, supervised teaching practice and the examination of "data" gathered in classrooms. Again if video cameras and playback facilities are available, these may increase the effectiveness of the course.

iii) purpose of the course: some are voluntary in the sense that participants sign up for them if they wish to. Others are obligatory, either because participants cannot begin as EFL teachers until the qualification in question has been gained, or because it falls within the terms of a practising teacher's contract with his or her employer (as is the case in short courses run by some education authorities). Apart from this, some courses, whether initial or in-service, aim to assist teachers to cope with TEFL across a range of teaching situations, while others focus on a specific context, or aim to bring about premeditated changes in classroom practice, for example when new teaching materials are being introduced to a school system or when there is a new syllabus implying a methodological shift to more "communicative" classroom work.

iv) funding: if participants are paying their own course fees and these monies are used directly to staff and resource the course, organisation motivation and impact may be different from courses where participants are "sponsored" or courses for which funding is "indirect" (or non-existent).

Criteria for selection of EFL teacher educators

The purpose of the foregoing deceptively simplistic overview is to provide a background against which to outline the main criteria that need to be considered when new staff are being sought to assist with or to take responsibility for teacher-education programmes in EFL. In Fig. 1 I represent the main criteria as a set of interrelated continua.

Experience of TEFL

short (e.g. 2 years) ←——————→ long

one teaching situation ←——————→ many teaching situations

one locality/country ←——————→ many localities/countries

one level (e.g. elementary) ←——————→ all levels

doesn't include experience ←——————→ includes a lot of
   parallel to trainees   parallel experience

teaching only ←——————→ teaching plus many duties

few teaching materials ←——————→ wide range of materials

only textbooks, board etc. ←——————→ wide range of resources
                           (e.g. video, lab, computers)

general EFL only ←——————→ EFL plus different types
                           of English for specific
                           purposes

no EFL teacher-training ←——————→ broad experience of teacher
   experience   training

Other experience

non-existent/narrow ←——————→ broad and varied

irrelevant to TEFL ←——————→ relevant to TEFL
   (e.g. truck-driving)   (e.g. other teaching)

Education, qualifications and personal skills

First degree only ←————————→ professional and post-graduate
                                                      qualifications

not specifically relevant ←————————→ relevant degree (e.g. English)
                                                      TEFL qualifications,
                                                      M.A. etc. "informing
                                                      disciplines" (e.g. psychology,
                                                      linguistics, education)

no background ←————————→ good background

knows only English ←————————→ knows several languages

intermediate English ←————————→ native-speaker English

grammar: no formal knowledge ←→ good formal knowledge

phonology: no knowledge ←————→ good knowledge

art; design; graphics: unskilled ←→ skilled in many media –

educational technology: most equipment

computing: and programming

voice & drama:

materials writing:

group management:

lecturing:

seminar-leading:

Personality and predominant teaching style

shy, reserved, quiet ←————————→ extrovert, sociable

consultative ←————————→ autocratic

neutral ←————————→ dynamic, energetic

carefully methodical ←————————→ unmethodical

gentle, approachable ←————————→ distant

teacher-centred ←————————→ learner-centred

very prone to anxiety ←————————→ unflappable

very self-aware ←————————→ not self-aware

committed to given ←————————→ uncommitted to any
    methodology   methodology

FIGURE 1   Some factors influencing the selection of teacher educators

Such an array of factors is daunting, to say the least, but it is intended only to indicate how different courses in different circumstances for different participants are likely to require different combinations of skills and characteristics. In the diagram above, it is not my purpose to imply that any particular characteristic or combination of characteristics is "best". Much will depend on the role the teacher educator will be assigned during the course, the course aims and the prevailing ideology. To give one example: on an initial training course (for example, one leading to the RSA Prep. Cert. TEFL), there might be some danger in selecting trainers who are unable to introduce, model or discuss techniques without exposing their own reservations about them. Initial trainees in most contexts need clear opportunities to master a repertoire of techniques for the classroom teaching of a foreign language that will enable them to survive and will provide a basis upon which they can develop, in due course, techniques that are their own and which conform to their own beliefs about language learning. Hesitant and ill-defined demonstrations and discussions which make the issues seem as complex and uncertain as they are in truth will not assist a majority of participants to acquire this repertoire. Conversely, if trainers are selected who are so committed to a given portfolio of techniques that their sole interest is to ensure that trainees have fully and slickly mastered them, the trainees may leave the course unable to adjust to new situations or to judge the appropriateness or otherwise of given techniques since time will not have been made available for proper discussion and evaluation, or practice in adapting technique to purpose.

Another important factor affecting selection of new teacher educators is the make-up and balance of the existing team. A majority of courses are given by teams of educators. It is crucial that members of the team should be able to work harmoniously and consistently together in planning, reviewing and administering the course. On the other hand, contrasts – though not conflicts – of style, personality and points of view are often helpful, particularly on in-service courses. What participants have most difficulty in coping with, however, is evidence of lack of consultation, conflicting information, and contradictory advice.

After selection, what then?

It is clearly not the case that staff, however suitable, can be plunged headlong into responsibility for a component to teacher education.

Among other things, the future members of the teacher education team will require:

i) opportunities to be involved in discussion of the rationale behind the course and the constraints surrounding the planning of it.

ii) familiarisation with the profiles of the course participants; as implied in the list above, it is clearly desirable for teacher educators to have experience within the teaching situation which course participants come from and/or will find themselves in after the course. If they do not, as may be the case with expatriate teacher-educators working in a new environment, there is a strong argument for organising means for them to acquire at least some relevant experience before or while taking on responsibilities related to the course.

iii) opportunities to observe colleagues and to work alongside them on all components of the course; this may include "training practice" in which the new educators try their hand at a given type of session for a short period and then discuss what happened with a more experienced colleague who has observed the session.

iv) involvement in day-to-day planning, administration, and materials selection and development; it is important that new team members should begin as soon as possible to share in background work so that their own thinking can develop alongside their responsibilities, and so that whatever new talents and slants they are able to contribute can emerge and be built on quickly.

v) regular opportunities to review the course, the progress of participants and the educators' own performance.

Keeping in touch with teaching

One of the biggest problems teacher educators face is maintaining a simultaneous role as teachers. For this reason, many establishments shun the notion of establishing staff as only responsible for teacher education, preferring instead to ensure that staff involved in teacher education rotate back into teaching after a given period or keep some classroom teaching alongside their teacher education duties. This is crucial, not just in school situations but also at university level, where teacher educators run the risk of completely losing touch with the first-hand experience of coping with full responsibility for real learners in real learning environments using up-to-date materials. The difficulty is that many university departments responsible for teacher education in EFL do not have the means of ensuring that staff maintain this contact and perhaps, through administrative and other requirements, make it difficult for them to do so.

Conclusion

I have tried to propose a clear if not exhaustive set of criteria for ensuring that staff selected to be involved in teacher education are fully able to respond to the immense responsibilities implied. I am, of course, aware that any such proposal is likely to remain just that, since the pressures and constraints of running teacher education programmes, often in financially unfavourable circumstances, make compromises and corner-cutting inevitable. However, a strong case can be made out for institutions developing their own much more specific checklists of criteria and their own ideal induction programmes so that, when new staff are required, the gap between what should ideally happen and what actually happens can be clearly seen and faced up to, and so that, when possible, steps can be taken to improve the situation for future generations of course participants.

11 This article looks at one of the key issues in teacher educa-
tion/training: who trains the trainers? It presents an outline of the
training programme which is used at International House for the
preparation of its trainers and of a course which has been designed
to meet this need generally for experienced EFL teachers and
educational administrators.

Just as twenty-five years ago, there was very little teacher-
training activity easily accessible in TEFL, so today there are
not many opportunities for the preparation of teacher educators
and trainers. The great majority of trainers simply begin as
experienced teachers – and sometimes not even with all that
much experience. In some parts of the world, the fact of being a
native-speaker teacher may lead to one finding oneself involved
in "teacher training". There is however today perhaps a sharper
awareness of the need to develop opportunities in this area than
there was twenty-five years ago of the need to train EFL teachers.
The starting point of being a teacher with ideas and experience to
share is by no means a bad one: as Donald Freeman has remarked:
"Teacher training is a fact of life: just about anyone who has been
teaching for a while has played the impromptu role of teacher
trainer in one form or another." But the base of experience needs
frameworks and contexts within which it can be profitably applied
to the preparation and development of teachers.

The Preparation and Development of
Teacher Trainers

TONY DUFF

Trainers must be teachers

Teacher training began at International House twenty-five years ago,
as a result of a pressing, urgent practical need: the need to find teachers.
The most effective way of answering this need seemed to be to set up a
training course that would meet the needs of the institution. As this
training course met with greater and greater success, as it met needs
beyond those of the immediate institution by starting to serve as a career
training for people wanting to teach EFL in many different places in the
world, and to be a source of trained teachers for other institutions and
organisations with the problem of how to find trained teachers of EFL
who would be effective in the classroom – it in turn, was confronted
with the problem of its own success. For as the demand for training in

EFL grew, so did the need for trainers, and the question of where to find them arose.

The answer was that they should be developed from within the existing teaching staff. By looking to the resource of the teaching staff, some of the fundamental tenets about teacher training were established. The first of these is that those who are training and attempting to develop teachers should themselves be currently practising classroom teachers, always in touch with learners and the daily problems facing the teacher and have first-hand experience with the most recent materials.

One of the inadequacies of much teacher-training activity throughout the world is that the trainers actively stop being teachers, and are training others to do something that they themselves no longer do. It is only common sense that you should practise what you preach, – but training of others must be grounded in one's own practice and not in some desiccated prescription deriving from almost forgotten – and even sometimes very limited – experience.

Theory application and practice

A second key tenet is that training – as indeed the word itself implies – should be practical and directly applicable to the working context. "Training" is now seen as a limited – and possibly limiting – word that runs the risk of offering a range of techniques and procedures that may be no more than a bag of tricks. If understood in such restricted terms, the idea of training will indeed be inadequate. It must embrace the wider concepts involved in teacher education and teacher development. Just as the most effective teachers have instinctively and always integrated communicative elements into their work, so have alert and sensitive trainers always been aware of the need to allow teachers to develop their own styles and approaches to teaching and to leave room for the broader human concerns involved in education and development. "Technique" as such is an illusion.

If a key tenet is that training should be practical and that the limitations inherent in the term be acknowledged and guarded against, it must be acknowledged that all practice is based on theory whether knowingly or unknowingly. "Good teaching practice is based on good theoretical understanding. There is indeed nothing so practical as a good theory." (Wardhaugh R. 1969 'TESOL: Current problems and classroom practices.' TESOL Quarterly). It is also worth noting that this word "theory" – which we think of in connection with reasoning comes, as the anthropologist Jane Harrison pointed out long ago, "from the same Greek word as theatre and means 'really looking fixedly at'; it is very near in meaning to our 'contemplation'." Contemplation of, reflection about what we do as practitioners and why – and about what we might do – are the essence of what lies at the root of a practical approach to training.

Another major feature of a practical approach to the training of teachers is that the trainers should use their skills as teachers when training. This is not to say that handling a group of trainee teachers is the same as working with a group of EFL students. There are of course differences – one of the most notable being the simple fact that trainees, whether native or non-native speakers, have a command of the language which allows them much more easily to challenge either what the trainer is proposing or the way of handling the group, which results in a different working relationship. Another striking difference is that as a teacher you may be aware in an unformulated way about why you do certain things, but as a trainer you must be able not only to explain what you do but exactly why you do it. "To be a teacher, you must know the technique. To be a trainer, you must know the technique, know why it is effective, be able to articulate or convey that understanding to others, and know how it relates to other aspects of language teaching." (Freeman, D. June, 1987, TESOL Newsletter Vol XXI No. 3 'Moving from Teacher to Teacher Trainer'.) The opportunities for using teaching skills in a training context are evident: the need to involve, to stimulate and motivate, to have clear manageable objectives, to ensure that what you intend to deal with can be accommodated within the time available, and so on.

The idea that as a result of a process of individual and group reflection on classroom teaching there can be a transfer of these insights to the training situation by using ways of teaching that have proved their effectiveness has been one of the cornerstones of this philosophy of teacher training.

Training the trainers

The assumptions about the staffing of courses that have just been outlined here led to a well-established programme of training for trainers. The programme is based on the master-apprentice model with additional support systems. The point of entry, generally, to this training is through the micro-teaching practice context. (The question of the selection of staff for teacher training/education, which is of great importance and significance, is not dealt with here. But see Richard Rossner, "Selecting Teacher Educators", page 101). A trainee trainer is attached to a teaching practice tutor and observes this tutor giving feedback to trainees over the period of a complete course. During this observation time, there are opportunities for discussion with the tutor and others working on the course, and the trainee trainer's perception is developed through work-sheets and tasks designed to help focus the process of observation and giving feedback, a delicate and difficult task (see Peter Maingay, "Observation for Training Development or Assessment?").

Those in training need to gain considerable experience at teaching practice since it is probably the most difficult area in terms of developing the trainer's perception and of enabling him/her to foster self-critical perception in the trainees themselves; the difficulty is all the greater because of the task of developing the ability to give constructive feedback sensitively. (For an overview of the progress of a trainer in training, see the schema on page 114.)

The work of trainers in training is supervised and monitored by the Director of Studies for teacher training and other senior staff. This too is a delicate exercise in communication, shaping of perception, and giving clear direction. Trainee trainers, like any learners involved in acquiring skills and knowledge, move at different rates, and this is allowed for. At a point when the individual trainer-in-training and the supervisor consider that the right moment has been reached to start giving lectures, seminars and workshops on training courses, this move is made. Often, though by no means invariably, the novice trainer starts by presenting sessions on aspects of language and phonology. The areas selected, however, are negotiated in relation to where the individual's interests and strengths lie and to the topics which the principal tutor working on the course wants to share.

Whilst this "input" contribution is developed, the trainee trainer continues to take teaching practice and to explore the relationship between "input" and its "carry through" effect to the trainees' application in the classroom. This stage of training continues until both trainee and supervisor consider that the right moment for movement to the final stage has been reached. The final stage involves the novice trainer taking responsibility for all aspects of the teacher-training course – lectures and seminars, teaching practice, co-ordination of trainees and the two other tutors who will normally be working on the course. As has been said, trainers develop at their own rate and according to their experience; this programme normally takes a minimum of six to fifteen months.

In addition to this essentially master/apprentice scheme of training and development, there is opportunity for informed exchange of ideas and sharing of preoccupations with the other tutors working on the course and with colleagues involved in other teacher-training courses: this is extremely valuable particularly in providing "reality checks" for trainers in training – there is no risk of feeling isolated and there are always colleagues to whom one can go for confirmation and validation – or help with getting back on the right track if one has strayed unprofitably.

At a more formal level, regular meetings are held within the teacher training department on all aspects of the work; a series of seminars will sometimes be run on topics that are a particular source of concern to

---

Schema of training process (Following selection for training)

STAGE 1	Observation of Teaching Practice (guided by the use of task sheets and checklists).	Discussion with tutor in charge and initial practice in writing feedback notes for trainee teachers.
	Taking teaching practice as tutor responsible for a group (several groups over a period of months).	Development of giving feedback both oral and written.
STAGE 2	Observation of "input" sessions.	Discussion with other tutors and colleagues together with use of materials designed for presentation of topics.
	Giving seminars, lectures and workshops in different areas of the syllabus.	
STAGE 3	Observation of all aspects of a course.	Final stage includes working with the teacher training administrative office on aspects of administration internal to the course.
	Taking responsibility for above and giving about two thirds of the total "input".	

All stages involve supervision (sitting in and feedback) by the Director of Studies (teacher training).

some trainers at a particular time or stage of their development, e.g. approaches to language analysis or handling of feedback with trainees. There is also a large range of material (task sheets, checklists, reading matter) to help the trainee trainer's process of development.

It is questionable whether taking teaching practice is the best starting point for a new trainer since it is undoubtedly the most difficult aspect, and depends for its success on experience as much as knowledge. However, were trainers to start by observing "input" sessions at the very beginning of their teacher-training activities, especially if such observation were to be of an entire course as it would probably need to be for the "input" devised to be appropriate to teaching practice, by the time they were approaching being responsible for their own course, they would undoubtedly feel the need for a second observation of the whole programme, which would add very considerably to the cost of training people to be trainers. (Obviously, all teacher education is a highly labour intensive *service* and the relationship between cost to the institution and fees is a factor which affects what can be done.)

Development of a course for trainers

This kind of training, based on a master/apprentice model, to prepare teacher-training staff (and sometimes for employees of other organisations, including the British Council) has been in use for many years. It has obviously only been possible to use with staff who have been selected to go into teacher training. As the demand for properly prepared teachers of English as a foreign language increases throughout the world, so does the need for trainers, and therefore for programmes and courses which will prepare them. To meet this need, a course has been designed to "train trainers". This course – the Teacher Trainer Development Course – has as its leitmotif the key issue of whether training has any effect and if so, in which circumstances? It explores the relationship between training and education. Everything that is discussed and read during the course is related to this point of departure and to how, from the training of trainers point of view, priorities can be established.

Two principal topic areas determine the overall programme for the course:

1. *Approaches to "input"*   2. *Approaches to observation of teachers*

- giving/leading seminars
- the use of teacher training handbooks
- devising handouts for specific groups
- devising ways of exploring video

- approaches to syllabus design (both *in-service programmes* and *course-based*).

- models of supervision
- approaches to oral/written feedback
- guiding observation

- developing trainee self-appraisal skills
- the fine line between encouragement and explicit feedback of weaknesses

Participants observe "live" sessions on training courses running currently (for both native and non-native speakers) and "live" teaching practice. They also get the opportunity of experience giving feedback to experienced teachers, doing EFL courses. In addition, there is practice in presentation work and each participant prepares a seminar pack for presenting within the group.

The course has been developed by again using the activities and resources within an institution's day-to-day work and aims to provide applied trainers/development opportunities from a basis of sound principles.

Conclusion

For many EFL teachers, movement into teacher training is at once a career development and a new stimulus. It is almost thought of as a kind of promotion although there are dangers in this idea, not least that it runs the risk of giving substance to the idea that the training of teachers is a somehow higher level process. It is an area of activity for which it is very difficult to get any formal preparation. The training programme and the course that are described above aim to provide such preparation. Such activities inevitably raise the question of "who trains the trainers?" It has been remarked that "there is a risk of infinite regress here". This is true, but what can be said with confidence is that those who undertake the preparation of teachers must themselves be teachers of wide experience, who continue to teach having become trainers and educators, and do not lose touch with the very activity they are preparing others for.

Acknowledgement

I would like to thank Martin Parrott, who designed the syllabus for the Teacher Training Development Course, and Ruth Gairns, who was the tutor in charge of the first such course, for discussing their work with me.

12 Peter Maingay writes about the different roles of observation in the training and development of teachers. Observation – "sitting in" as it was known at International House in the early years – has become a contentious issue for many teachers in all fields of education. This is understandable; it is almost always inextricably connected in the minds of teachers with assessment since their formative experience of observation will have been in the assessment/training context of preparatory courses.

Observation produces feelings of anxiety in teachers because of this question of assessment and their "performance" being judged. Some, however, resent it on the grounds that it is intrusive and that other professionals are not subject to such "policing". Although the teaching profession is unusual in being able to carry on its activities behind closed doors; there is a sense in which surgeons, say, are observed (by colleagues) all the time, not to mention performers of any kind. Significantly, the observer very often experiences as much anxiety about the responsibility of passing judgement. As we have become more aware of the complex interaction of factors involved in teaching and of the difficulties of establishing reliable criteria for saying whether the process has been successful or not, there is great reluctance to make judgements.

The tradition of "the open classroom" has from the beginning been one of the founding principles of teacher training and development at International House. John Haycraft speaks of the enthusiasm with which teachers welcomed observation as a stimulus to reflection and development (see page 7).

Teachers – both the observed and the observer – and learners must be involved in the process if reflection is to be illuminating. Observation flourishes in an atmosphere in which it is regarded as unexceptional, as something which happens often because colleagues are involved in developing, in sharing experience, and approaches to solving problems in the classroom.

Observation for Training, Development or Assessment?

PETER MAINGAY

1. Introduction: ritual and principle

I want to begin by trying to define what will be a leitmotif of this article: the distinction between "ritual teaching behaviour" and "principled teaching behaviour". By ritual teaching behaviour I mean teaching that is unthinking; that is, or has become, divorced from the principles that lie behind it. It is teaching behaviour that is either purely imitative; or it is teaching behaviour that has set into patterns that no longer reveal awareness on the teacher's part of why he or she should be teaching in that particular way. This kind of teaching is ritual in the sense that, although there may be principles behind it, the teacher has never known, or has lost sight of, those principles, and is consequently going through the motions in the same way as a child will recite multiplication tables. This kind of teaching behaviour, as I shall suggest below, has its value, but is not generative in the way that principled teaching behaviour is. I shall use the term "principled teaching behaviour" to describe teaching that is informed by principles that the teacher is aware of. By "principles", I do not necessarily mean anything particularly abstract or difficult: the principles may quite simply be "the reasons for doing something".[1]

Much of what a teacher does in a language-teaching classroom is ritual behaviour rather than principled behaviour; and I believe that the most important role of an observer in most, if not all, observations is that of making teachers think about what they do: of drawing their attention to the principles behind the rituals, of leading them away from ritual behaviour towards principled behaviour. In order to approach this distinction, let's first look at a parallel between speaking and teaching. In speaking, much of what we say is automatic, in that we do not need to actively choose words. Quite a large proportion of a native speaker's spoken language will consist of formulaic expressions, which the speaker will produce without any effort, without having to choose them consciously; only a small proportion will be carefully chosen to suit that particular utterance. The fact that we do not consciously have to create a large part of what we say leaves us free to process what we hear more efficiently and to be creative when we wish, or need, to be. In other words, these formulaic expressions, of which every native speaker has thousands, enable us to cope with fluent conversation in a way we could not if we had to invent anew everything we said.[2]

Similarly an EFL teacher – or any teacher for that matter – possesses a stock of techniques or procedures which he/she does not have to think about. Starting a class, correcting spoken error, arranging pair or group work, pre-teaching lexis, writing new lexis on the board with accompanying stress marks – the list could be endless – rapidly become rituals that can be performed without conscious thought. And just as formulaic expressions free a speaker to focus on other things, so such classroom rituals enable teachers to gain some respite from the strain of teaching 25 classes a week, and free them to pay close attention to other matters in a lesson.

However, there are two dangers in this use of ritual behaviour in class: in one situation a new teacher, just off a pre-service training course, may have picked up such rituals very efficiently, having watched his/her trainer or other experienced teachers perform them. This is obviously an important part of initial training, probably a *sine qua non*; but it is essential that at a fairly early point in that teacher's career, the principles behind the rituals are made clear to him or her in some way, so that rituals can generate fresh behaviour. We will look at this in more detail later. And in another situation, a more experienced teacher, who had a principled knowledge of his teaching, who has at some point chosen certain techniques for principled reasons, has lost sight of those reasons and his teaching has consequently set into unquestioned ritual. Again, I will give examples of this later, when we come to the role of the observer as developer, as opposed to trainer.

2. Four reasons for observing

Having looked at the background to what I consider to be the most valuable role of the observer, that of developer, I want to turn to reasons for observing.

First of all, teachers are observed, particularly in pre-service situations, for training purposes.[3] They are observed trying out some of the procedures they themselves have observed or been told about and, as a result of this observation, they will receive fairly directive feedback – prescriptive criticism that will tell them fairly precisely what they are doing right and what they are doing wrong. In a variety of ways, they will be guided towards more appropriate classroom behaviour than they have displayed. Such observation and feedback is perhaps most typically, but by no means exclusively, seen on an RSA Preparatory TEFL course or on a pre-service training course within a state education system.

Secondly, teachers are observed for assessment purposes. Assessment will take place either pre-service or in-service, as part of a course or outside a course, by an assessor from within or from outside the institution for which the teacher observed is working. The type of observation – is the assessor looking for details or for global impressions? Is he or she looking at one lesson or a series of lesson? Is the assessment one that involves feedback and discussion or not? All this will vary enormously, as will the type of feedback, (if there is any). Such observation, involving some type of assessment, may happen within a language school, where the observer may be the Director of Studies;

it may happen on a teacher-training course, where the assessor may be an external inspector provided by the Ministry of Education; or it may happen on a course where the assessor is provided by the examining body, as on the RSA Dip. TEFLA scheme.

Thirdly, teachers are observed for development purposes.[3] They are observed in their place of work or on an in-service course where the main focus will be on re-examining what has been taken for granted, on developing skills of self-appraisal rather than on learning new teaching skills, though the latter will not necessarily be ignored. Where development is the main purpose of observation, the observer may provide less directive feedback than when the purpose of observation is primarily training. The feedback will involve guidance, suggestion and exchange of ideas; but above all, the observer will be leading the observed teacher towards self-appraisal (including looking afresh at behaviour that may have become ritual) and towards developing new ideas for herself/himself. An observer, when involved in observing for training, will be providing scaffolding to support a new teacher; but when involved in observation for development he or she will be dismantling that scaffolding so that the teacher can stand on his own.

Finally, teachers are observed for observer development purposes. By this I do not mean the observer is being trained as an observer (though this too is an important element of all four types of observation I have mentioned), but that the observer is there because he/she wants to pick up new ideas, or wants an opportunity to reflect on teaching through watching someone else. This is only likely to happen amongst peers, in a school where time is available for such activities – a rare, but very much to be encouraged situation. In this situation, feedback, if there is any, will be informal and will most likely involve the observer reflecting on what he or she got out of the lesson that was of value. I shall not be considering this type of observation in this article.

Before moving on to consider in more detail observation for development, and later observation for assessment, I should make it clear that the four categories of observation I have mentioned are not exhaustive: my categorisation is only one way of dividing up, and therefore getting to grips with, a large area. And more importantly, my four categories are not discrete: quite clearly, there is considerable overlap (see Figure 1). It will be a rare occasion that an observation is training pure and simple, or development alone. Only observation as pure assessment might occur regularly. Otherwise, most observations will include elements of training, development, assessment and observer development – though the latter may be unacknowledged! I would go further and say that all observation should contain elements of development for the observed teacher: and it is this that I shall focus on in the next section.

FIGURE 1:   Four categories of observation

3. Observation for training and development

I have brought training and development together in this section, not only because, as mentioned in the previous section, the two obviously overlap and intermingle; but also because observation for training should contain the seeds of observation for development. This is because pre-service training will often involve teachers in imitating recipes, in establishing rituals that allow them to cope in what are often very nerve-wracking circumstances. But those rituals should not be allowed to set into fossilised teaching behaviour, behaviour that betrays no knowledge of the principles behind the behaviour: it is one of the duties of an observer on a pre-service training course to start trainee teachers off on a development path. It is this that I shall look at first in this section.[4]

What matters in observation is what the observer chooses to take note of with a view to providing either written feedback or oral feedback – or both – and then how that feedback is provided. So an observer may notice that a trainee teacher on a pre-service course stays quietly out of the way while the class is working in pairs, having set the activity up clearly and efficiently; but while the students are working in pairs – and having some difficulty – the teacher is looking at his lesson plan and a little later, when one pair evidently wants help, the teacher says "No, you're working on your own; wait until everyone's finished, then I'll help." The observer writes the following (the notes are intended for the trainee teacher):

– good: you stayed out of the limelight while the class was working in pairs

– don't, however, cut out altogether: looking at your lesson plan meant you weren't paying attention to how and what students were doing. You should at least keep your ears pricked up for the mistakes they're making, and watch out for students in difficulty . . .
– and indeed, one pair had to call for help, and you didn't hear for a while – then you refused help. This was probably not the best thing to do. Why not help them? If you don't they just go silent and don't complete the activity. Don't carry teacher non-involvement too far!

These notes are typical of judgemental and directive observation: they tell the teacher what was good and what was not good, and inform him fairly firmly about what should and should not be done. Such notes are very useful for a teacher in pre-service training. But an alternative – and I think preferable, in developmental terms – way of providing written feedback might look like this:

– you set the pair work activity up well
What did you do while the activity was going on? Can you remember? One pair asked for help and you told them to wait until everyone had finished? Why? Was this decision based on something I have told you in input? If so, what? Are there circumstances when a possible "rule" or technique I have suggested to you for behaviour (by you) during pair or group work might not apply?
What might those circumstances be?

This may seem a lot for an observer to write while watching a lesson, but as all experienced observers will know, it is amazing how skilled one becomes at writing at the same time as listening and watching. There are three important points to make about the second of the above extracts from an observer's notes:

1. The number of questions would depend firstly on the amount of time available for oral feedback after the lesson – if there were a lot of time, then some of the questions might be discussed and the observer could ask correspondingly more questions on the feedback sheet and secondly on the stage of training – the longer the trainee has been receiving this kind of feedback the more questions could be put to him/her.

2. Any teacher under regular observation needs some kind of tuning in to the kind of feedback he or she is going to get. In this case, the observer, as part of the course, would outline the underlying reasons for this kind of approach, and would make the point that many of the questions asked do not imply criticism of the teaching, but are simply

intended to make the trainee think about what lies behind the decisions made in class.

3. What the observer was getting at, in this instance I suspect, was that the trainee, having been told that students need time to work on their own, when the teacher is out of the way, was carrying out "instructions" to the letter, and was not prepared to go against those instructions despite the fact that two students clearly needed guidance. In other words, this teacher was making a small part of his teaching behaviour a ritual, perhaps without being aware of the principles behind the ritual; but more importantly, in this case he was unaware of a greater principle – that any guideline, from the trainer, or set of procedures, can be deviated from in certain circumstances.[5]

In other words, in the second extract above, the observer is asking the trainee teacher to look more closely at what he did at that point in the lesson, and to consider why he did it, so that the trainee does not fall into an unquestioned pattern of behaviour, a ritual for his role during pair work; and more generally, the observer is involved in developing the trainee teacher's awareness of teaching, and the trainee's skills of self-appraisal. This aspect of the observer's job is crucial, regardless of the degree of experience of the observed teacher. In this instance, on a pre-service training course, the observer is acting to prevent taught procedures fossilising into set patterns: she is, in as non-directive a way as possible[6], pointing the trainee along the open road to development, a road that should lead out of the narrow (but necessary) alley of training.

Now I turn to observation at a stage when a teacher is well beyond initial training: in-service observation of an experienced teacher, whether on a course or simply teaching an ordinary lesson as part of his or her daily schedule.

Assuming that the teacher wants the observer to be there, and welcomes the presence of someone who will comment positively, the observer might make the following notes during a part of the lesson in which the teacher was dealing with students producing language they either weren't sure about or were using incorrectly. On page 125 is an edited section of notes – some intervening comments have been omitted; the numbers are provided for ease of reference when observer and observed discuss the lesson.

The format of these notes is moving towards the format of a worksheet. The observer and the observed teacher may simply use the notes as a prompt for discussion and the blank column could be used by the teacher to scribble notes in; or he/she may choose to use it later when he/she reflects on the discussion, as a way of consolidating or developing any thoughts that have arisen as a result of the discussion.

> (6)   You elicited "What does he look like?" well. How else could you have introduced the target structure?
>
> (7)   Is it always a good policy not to give new words in writing first? Are there arguments *for* writing up new words first? If so, what are they?
>
> (8)   What danger lurks in providing "He looks like a businessman" as a possible answer in a dialogue designed to introduce "What does he look like?"
>
> (14)   Quite a few English loanwords were coming out – playboy, showman, topmodel. What problems might these words cause?
>
> (19)   You tried to explain "shy". What else could you have done to get the meaning across?
>
> Is explanation the only method? The best method? *Is* there a "best method"? Or does your choice of "method" depend on circumstances? If so, what are the circumstances, the factors involved?

A third possibility would be for the discussion not to take place for a day, allowing the teacher time to reflect on the issues brought up by the observer, and to write in possible reactions to the observer's questions. And a final possibility, particularly when time for discussion is short, would be for the observed teacher to use the observer's notes as a straight worksheet.

The question in point (6) and one of the questions in point (19) are "alternative" questions. The observer is not saying "What you did was wrong", but is using the observation as a way of encouraging the teacher to think of alternatives. Ideally, these would be discussed, as would the implications of the alternatives in (7)[7]. I feel that these "What else?" or "How else?" questions, as well as the other types of questions (as in points (7), (8), (14) and (19)) serve an important developmental purpose: they encourage a teacher to think constantly of achieving aims in different ways. This is desirable not because change for change's sake is necessarily always right, but because a teacher often needs to avoid getting into a rut, in which, because the way he/she teaches is no longer fresh for him/her, the students are no longer benefiting from teaching that is stimulatingly close to its source. Just as idioms become style and lose their original value, so certain teaching procedures lose touch with their origins and fade into weak parrotting – parrotting by the teacher, that is. They become ritual behaviour whose links with the principles that originally informed that behaviour have been severed. Before I give an example, I should go back to a point I made in the first section, when I drew a parallel between formulaic expressions in language and a teacher's stock of techniques for the language-teaching classroom. Those techniques, or procedures, are learned at an early stage – and at that stage, the danger is that the principles behind the techniques are not understood, so the techniques are enacted as lip-service ritual. In a way, this is acceptable, since every teacher needs these techniques, perhaps in a fairly automatic form, to release him or her to think freshly about other aspects of a lesson.

These procedures are the formulaic expressions of the classroom. As a teacher develops, however, he or she questions these procedures, perhaps dismantles them in the light of new understanding of the principles behind them before re-integrating into his or her teaching with the aid of new insights and perhaps new techniques as well. It is after this stage – a stage a teacher will reach many times in his or her career – that principled, fresh teaching behaviour sets into ritual again.

I recently observed a teacher, with 4 years' teaching behind him, on an RSA Dip. TEFLA course. He had presented the second conditional, used to express hypotheses, as in "What would you do if you were stranded on a desert island?" He wanted to provide students with an opportunity to ask and answer questions, made up by them, using this new language. He gave out grids for them to fill in, looking like this:

Your questions	Answers		
	Name	Name	Name

and then quickly told the students what to do. They proceeded to write questions like "What would you do if you were a teacher?" "What would you do if you were rich?" "What would you do if you had a holiday now?", and then circulated, asking and answering and filling in their grids. Finally, the teacher asked for a few sample questions and answers. Now it is true that the students did get practice of the new language, and there was some kind of information gap. But there was no reason for asking and answering, except that they were playing the game that students play most of the time: do what teacher asks as he or she probably knows best. But the activity was little more than a mechanical drill, in effect, and the students would have got almost as much practice if they had done a fairly meaningless written exercise. I am perhaps being a little harsh, but that was the impression I got as an observer, and it was the impression the students' rather bored behaviour gave – and the teacher's, come to that. But he knew all about communicative language teaching; if he'd been asked, he would have given all the right answers to such questions as, "Why do you try to set up situations in which students have a genuine need to communicate with each other?" "Why do you try to provide students with an opportunity to talk about something of interest and relevance to themselves?" "Why do you ask students to work in pairs some of the time?" "Why do you try to place controlled practice in as appropriate a context as possible?" "Why do you pay attention to the appropriate use of language?" In other words, the principled knowledge was there, but the manifestations of that knowledge – what he asked the students to do in class – had become divorced from that knowledge and had turned into ritual. To use another analogy: the function of this stage of his lesson – providing students with an opportunity to practise newly-learnt language in a relatively communicative context – was being expressed by an exponent – making up questions to ask other students in class, and then asking them – that had lost its freshness and was conducted with little interest on the teacher's part, and consequently the students' part. It is, then, one of the observer's roles to alert a teacher to such behaviour and its consequences and to make him or her aware of the need for regular examination of what has become ritual.

4. Observation for assessment

The two chief effects of observation for assessment take an extreme form of what happens in any observation: the teacher feels threatened and nervous, and the lesson tends to be a one-off display, an isolated performance, too little related to the lessons surrounding the assessment lesson. A third is the backwash effect that the presence of a practical assessment has on any teacher-training course: the way the practical component of a course is taught and received will be influenced considerably by the trainer's and the trainees' perceptions of the requirements of the practical assessment.

We will never wholly escape the first effect, the affective one. An additional presence in any group, whether inside a classroom or outside, will alter the behaviour of the group and the individuals; in a classroom the presence of an outsider who is not involved in any way cannot but affect the behaviour of the students and of the teacher. Observation classrooms, with one-way glass walls, are a rarity; audio-recording does not provide enough data[8]; video-recording is better, but returns us to the problem we're trying to avoid – the presence of outsiders in the classroom. So clearly there is no getting away from an observer's presence. Instead we must search for ways to reduce the effects of that presence.

The second area in which assessment affects teaching is perhaps of greater consequence than the first, though the teacher under assessment may not agree with this sentiment at the time. Assessment of teachers tends to focus on one lesson: this, not surprisingly, leads to an unhealthy emphasis on displaying teaching skills for one lesson only. Longer term planning, timetabling, planning sequences of lessons – all are neglected (though not totally ignored) at the expense of the lesson and the lesson plan. This cannot be beneficial. It may be necessary to develop the necessary skills to cope with one lesson; but just as at a lower level, mastering techniques and procedures is necessary but not sufficient, so too, being able to teach a lesson is obviously essential, but by no means enough. It is not enough for two reasons: first, lessons are not isolated events. They are part of a process, and should no more be the unit of assessment than, say, a 10-minute chunk of a lesson. Second, the teacher being assessed can get away with – and will often be graded highly for – a fireworks display of techniques, very little of which will be beneficial to the students. What is done in the lesson need have little or no connection with the lesson before or the lesson to come for the assessor to judge it a pass, or a "good lesson", or evidence of a teacher's employability, etc. Equally, the teacher can put on a fairly routine performance – fireworks maybe, but still routine in the sense I have been using the word in this article – without having to display any knowledge of the principles behind the routine.

So, what can be done to improve conditions of assessment? In the context of a training course, a number of steps can be taken[9]. I shall illustrate these steps by describing a possible scheme for an RSA Diploma TEFLA course. First of all, participants on the course need to be clear about the reasons for the particular scheme of observation, feedback and assessment: without understanding and, as far as it is possible, approval of those reasons and of the scheme, a lot of its value will be lost. Just as we need to let our EFL students in on the reasons for some of our teaching procedures, so we need to canvas the support and active involvement of our trainees by giving them as much background information as possible. If this leads to discussion and disagreement, then a negotiated compromise should be reached.

Secondly, feedback sheets of the kind shown on pages 122 and 123 should be used from the beginning of the course, with an accompanying focus on a) prodding for alternative teaching procedures and b) prodding for reasons behind behaviour, rather than simple comment and criticism (though the latter will by no means be excluded).

Thirdly, these feedback sheets should be made use of in input sessions. They could provide the basis for a session on a first topic (for example, on teaching vocabulary, using the feedback sheets on page 125); or they could serve as backup in a recycling session (for example, on the teacher's role at various stages of a lesson, using the sheet illustrated on page 122/3).

Fourth, observation should be of sequences of lessons – and feedback, both written and oral, should reflect this. I remarked earlier on the fact that one lesson as a unit of observation (and assessment) is no more satisfactory than 10 minutes; one could, of course, argue that 5 lessons are no more satisfactory than one lesson. But if 5 lessons (or 7 or 9, etc) are observed (and assessed) in sequence, you are acknowledging that teaching and learning take place over long periods rather than short, relative though those adjectives may be. By observing a sequence of lessons, an observer will then be able to focus on – and draw a trainee's attention to – development, not just training: for training is more concerned with small effects, whereas development entails larger concerns – for the students, the development of reading skills over a period of time or the slow acquisition of meaning; and, in terms of trainee development, the gradual adjustment and fine-tuning of teaching skills, and the constant reassessment of habits and patterns of behaviour.

Fifthly, assessment should run right through a course and not be simply tacked onto the end. It should not consist of assessment of individual lessons, but of the development of a trainee over the whole course; it should focus chiefly on a trainee's awareness of alternatives, of principles behind teaching behaviour; and it should be tied in with a trainee's awareness of the way theory and practice are linked as shown in written work and oral contributions during input. In other words, there should be no dichotomy between theory and practice, between "the written" and "the practical".

Sixthly, observation for assessment should always be done by the course tutor – the person who, one hopes, makes the candidate feel most at ease. This should tie in with the seventh point: that observation for training and development and observation for assessment should be "a seamless garment". There should be no distinction between them. Some will say that this simply shifts the tension of one-off assessments to the whole course. This may be so, but the degree of tension experienced by some teachers for a one-off assessment cannot be maintained over a long period: I would argue that reduced tension, spread over a long period, coupled with the candidate's knowledge that everything is being taken into account, not just the skills displayed in class, must be preferable to a judgement based on one or two individual lessons.

Clearly, certain aspects of this scheme for observation and assessment on an RSA Diploma TEFLA course will not apply in other observation for assessment circumstances. But I would suggest that anyone involved in observation, whether for assessment or not, whether as part of a course or not, could benefit from taking on some of the attitudes I have been discussing.

I have called this article "Observation for Training, Development or Assessment?", and I have argued that observation is rarely for one purpose only, often for two and frequently – and most desirably – for all three: for training, development and assessment together, the presence of the third with the first two having the effect of reducing the negative side of observation for assessment. I have also suggested that one of the main purposes of observation should be to make observed teachers, at all stages in their careers, more aware of alternatives and more conscious of how teaching can set into unquestioned ritual. Perhaps I should conclude by pointing out the obvious – that promotion of constant examination of ritual can in itself become unthinking ritual behaviour on the part of observers: they too need constantly to monitor their own behaviour to ensure that principle always informs it.

Footnotes

1 Derek Edwards and Neil Mercer, on p. 97 of their book *Common Knowledge* (Methuen 1987), make the following comment: "Procedural knowledge becomes ritual where it substitutes for an understanding of underlying principles ... Principled knowledge is defined as essentially explanatory,

oriented towards an understanding of how procedures and processes work, of why certain conclusions are necessary or valid, rather than being arbitrary things to say because they seem to please the teacher." Although this description is of the behaviour of children in primary schools, much of it applies to the EFL teacher.

2 See the article by Pawley, A. and Syder, F. N. "Two Puzzles for Linguistic Theory: nativelike selection and nativelike fluency" in (ed. Richards J. C. and Schmidt R. W.) *Language and Communication* (Longman 1983).

3 "Training deals with building specific teaching skills: how to sequence a lesson or how to teach a dialogue, for instance. Development, on the other hand, focuses on the individual teacher – on the process of reflection, examination and change which can lead to doing a better job, and to personal and professional growth." (From Freeman D. TESOL Quarterly, March 1982).

4 Clearly, on any course that sets out to integrate theory and practice, and input and teaching practice, much of the development work will be done during input – lectures and discussion, reading etc. But it is my feeling that observation of teaching practice does not provide a strong enough link with input; inadequate feedback flows back into input.

5 The only principle for which no exception can be found might be the one that states "There are always circumstances in which a principle can be abandoned."

6 I admit that, at this early stage in particular, genuinely non-directive feedback is impossible and probably undesirable. (See Freeman D. op. cit.)

7 For further reading on the idea of generating alternatives, see Fanselow J. *Breaking Rules* (Longman 1987).

8 Though it is extremely useful for teacher's self-observation – another type of observation perhaps?

9 I choose to focus on the context of a training course, but much of what I suggest can be applied to assessment outside those bounds.